"JUST" A HOUSEWIFE

The Powerful Role that Shapes Generations

Ann Lindholm

Copyright © 2020

HIS Publishing House © 2020

COPYRIGHT

All scripture, unless otherwise noted, is from the Fire Bible: English Standard Version (ESV), published by Hendrickson Publishers Marketing. The Holy Bible, English Standard Version (ESV) Copyright © 2001 by Crossway Bibles, a publishing ministry of Good News Publishers. Quote marks, italics, bold print and capitalization added for emphasis and clarity and dually noted.

All rights reserved. No part of this publication may be reproduced, stored in a retrieval system, or transmitted in any form or by any means—electronic, mechanical, photocopy, recording, or any other—except for brief quotations in printed reviews, without the permission of the Author or Publisher.

Cover design © The Collaborative Press. Cover photos © Ashlyn Gunter. Edited by Amy Dohmen @ The Collaborative Press.
Ann Lindholm Copyright © 2020.
Library of Congress Control Number: 2020900146

"*Just*" *a Housewife* is available in digital and print format:
www.authorannlindholm.com

REVIEWS

Author Ann Lindholm offers a helpful and practical approach to homemaking tips and strategies in the following in her book *"Just" a Housewife*. Whether a seasoned veteran or a fresh newlywed, women of all generations will benefit from her no-nonsense approach. Large budgets and spacious homes have nothing to do with providing your family with a warm and welcoming home front. In fact, in the abundance of space and money we often find ourselves consumed by managing our "things" instead of managing our families. Like sitting down to share a cup of coffee with a friend, Ann provides anecdotal insight ranging from creating a family centered lifestyle to practical tips for daily and deep cleaning.

Don't be fooled by the title however, *"Just" a Housewife* easily pertains to women who work outside of the home as well. In a time where so many women are opposite sides of the fence, the author does a lovely job of sharing her viewpoint and advice without condemning the women who do it differently than her. All women, regardless of "SAHM" or "Working Mom" want the best for their families and their homes and would surely benefit from tips and insight in this book!

Lauren Grumbles, Designer
www.laurengrumbles.com

LAUREN GRUMBLES
INTERIOR DESIGN

CONTENTS

COPYRIGHT 2
REVIEWS 4
CONTENTS 6
ACKNOWLEDGEMENTS 7
FOREWORD 10
PROVERBS 31:10-31 14
INTRODUCTION 16
AS FOR ME AND MY HOUSE 23
SERVING YOUR HUSBAND 32
PROVERBS 31 WIFE 52
CREATIVELY CUTTING COSTS 59
RAISING DISCIPLES 66
HOME SCHOOLING 85
HOMEMAKING 102
CLEANLINESS AND ORGANIZATION 115
FAMILY HEALTH 132
HOSPITALITY 163
COOKING 169
FAVORITE RECIPES 189
MILITARY FAMILIES 228
RECOMMENDED RESOURCES 254
OTHER TITLES BY ANN LINDHOLM 255

ACKNOWLEDGEMENTS

Our home is run under the Lordship of Jesus Christ, so I must first recognize and acknowledge Him. If not for His example as the ultimate servant I would not have learned how to serve my family well. To Him be all the glory!

I also want to thank my mother, Judy Saladino, for showing me by example how to make a house a home. From my earliest ages I vividly remember her meticulously cleaning our home, maintaining the lawn, creating delicious meals and amazing desserts. She often made our home hospitable to company. To this day, my friends know that if you want to eat at the Saladino's home, you better be there by 6 o'clock (It may have changed to 5:30pm)! The food she made was incredible. She made our house a safe, comfortable place to live and love. I am so grateful for a mother who stayed home during my younger years and was always home when I returned from school with warm cookies and milk awaiting. It is from my mother I learned the importance of good housekeeping.

Most of all, I want to thank my amazing husband, whom I refer to as Hero. If it wasn't for him, I wouldn't have the opportunity to be a housewife. He has supported me from the very beginning. In fact, I remember before we got married he expressed the desire for me to remain home with our children and not wanting to have to rely on a daycare or someone else to raise them. I was especially grateful to be a housewife while he was deployed all those years. I am so appreciative of how hard he works to provide for our family, especially since we began home schooling. It means the world to us that he supports our home school efforts and at times teaches our children (albeit on military strategy and tactics!). After very long and hard days from work, he often comes home and plays ball with the kids and their friends outside, sometimes not even making it through the door! Because of my Hero's efforts, I am able to write this book. Baby, you're the greatest! Thank you! I love you!

Finally, I am so grateful for Ashlyn Gunter, my dear sister in Christ and friend. She not only made the photo shoot for the cover extremely fun, she did an amazing job with the photography. She has been so blessed with an eye for beauty and detail. Thank you so much Ashlyn!

FOREWORD

Pastor Joshua Gunter

The older I get, the more I realize the importance of discipleship. I do not simply mean evangelizing the lost or striving to convert individuals to Christianity. Though these things are important, we must remember a huge part of discipleship is training believers to live successfully.

The Apostle Paul, writing a letter to one of his spiritual sons, speaks on this subject. In Titus 2:1-5, Paul urges older men and women to teach the younger generation how to operate in their conduct. This is a practice that has been lost in many of our churches today. There has been a great separation between the younger and older generations. Yet, the Church is the family of God, not to be separated by economic or generational classes. In a family, the older, more mature members train up the next generation. Likewise, God has so arranged the Church to do the same. Titus 2:3-5 specifically says "Older women likewise are to be reverent in behavior, not slanderers or slave to much wine. They are to teach what is good, and so train the young women to love their husbands and children, to be self-controlled, pure, working at home, kind, and submissive to their own husbands, that the word of God may not be reviled." I believe that is exactly the goal of this book. To teach younger women in the sacred art of homemaking.

In her book, *Just a Housewife*, Ann Lindholm communicates very practical ways a young woman can prepare herself as she enters into the role of wife or mother. Her passion for family and discipleship is easily identified in each chapter.

I fully believe that next to Jesus Himself and His Spirit, the greatest gift God has ever given man is woman. Women and men were both designed by God and both fulfill very special roles in humanity. Our culture's concept of these roles has drifted away from what the Bible teaches about them. I am not saying that a woman shouldn't ever work outside the home or should be domineered by a man. What I am saying, is that there is a biblical separation in the roles of man and woman. Young men and young women are in desperate need of an elder taking them by the hand and teaching them everyday principles that are essential to fulfill God's calling and design for their lives.

Many feel it is old fashioned for a woman to stay at home and be a homemaker. Some believe that it belittles or demeans a woman, as if it is degrading for a wife/mother to work at home. As a man, husband, and father I am eternally grateful for the hard work my wife, Ashlyn, puts into our home! I have a great comfort in knowing that the love of my life, the woman whom I have become one with, is the one influencing and teaching my children and not some individual I barely know. Without her hard work, our house would be a disaster and our family would not function as smoothly as it does. I know that she has been designed to fulfill a role that I could never fill myself.

As you read *Just a Housewife*, maybe not everything in it will pertain to you and your circumstance. You may read something and have a different opinion on how to accomplish the same goal, but I encourage you to find ways you can better yourself as an individual by applying the information presented in this book with a humble spirit.

With brotherly affection,

Joshua Gunter,

Pastor of The Gathering-Springfield

PROVERBS 31:10-31

[10]An excellent wife who can find?
She is far more precious than jewels.
[11]The heart of her husband trusts in her,
and he will have no lack of gain.
[12]She does him good, and not harm,
all the days of her life.
[13]She seeks wool and flax,
and works with willing hands.
[14]She is like the ships of the merchant;
she brings her food from afar.
[15]She rises while it is yet night
and provides food for her household
and portions for her maidens.
[16]She considers a field and buys it;
with the fruit of her hands she plants a vineyard.
[17]She dresses herself with strength
and makes her arms strong.
[18]She perceives that her merchandise is profitable.
Her lamp does not go out at night.

¹⁹She puts her hands to the distaff,
and her hands hold the spindle.
²⁰She opens her hand to the poor
and reaches out her hands to the needy.
²¹She is not afraid of snow for her household,
for all her household are clothed in scarlet.
²²She makes bed coverings for herself;
her clothing is fine linen and purple.
²³Her husband is known in the gates
when he sits among the elders of the land.
²⁴She makes linen garments and sells them;
she delivers sashes to the merchant.
²⁵Strength and dignity are her clothing,
and she laughs at the time to come.
²⁶She opens her mouth with wisdom,
and the teaching of kindness is on her tongue.
²⁷She looks well to the ways of her household
and does not eat the bread of idleness.
²⁸Her children rise up and call her blessed;
her husband also, and he praises her:
²⁹"Many women have done excellently,
but you surpass them all."
³⁰Charm is deceitful, and beauty is vain,
but a woman who fears the Lord is to be praised.
³¹Give her of the fruit of her hands,
and let her works praise her in the gates.

INTRODUCTION

So often we hear statements that make housewives cringe…"Oh, you're just a housewife? What do you do with all that time? I wish I could just hang out at home all day."

Okay, let me set things straight right here and right now. Being "just" a housewife is probably the most difficult job I have ever had! I realize many songs have been made about this very subject. But let us talk about it from a faith-based position. Being a housewife is actually one of the most important roles a woman can hold.

A housewife carries a great burden and responsibility to raise children into men and women. To shape them into leaders and functioning adults in society. Yet, Hollywood and the world downplays this crucial role and even deceives women into believing housewives are no longer necessary or important. This could not be further from the truth. One only needs to look around the world and listen to news of all the brokenness. Look at the suicide rate among teens. What about teen drinking, drug use, and sex? Not to mention the whole LGBTQ....XYZ hysteria. Hollywood and society are pushing an agenda, leaving our children confused about their identities. It is very clear that there is a major breakdown within the home and family unit. When did this occur? I fully believe it entered the scene around the 1950's when women started participating in the workforce and the divorce rate jumped. It started entering the big screen on new sitcoms and movies, attempting to soften the hearts of America for what was to come. It especially sparked up in the 1970's during the "Women's Liberation" movement. We are suffering from the aftermath today.

We have fallen for great lies. The lie that worldly gain is more important than raising a godly family. The lie that women should work a full-time job outside of the home. The lie that women should be "equal" to men and carry the same burden of providing for, leading, and protecting the family. We have fallen for the very detrimental lie that being a stay-at-home wife and mom is not necessary.

We are plainly seeing the devastating results of a society that has fallen for these lies, and we haven't even touched on the subject of divorce and how it impacts our children.

There are times when the woman may work outside the home and the man raises the children and maintains the home. Yes, there are times both parents will work outside the home. I am not condemning that. What this book is NOT saying, is that you are less of a woman for not being a housewife. This book is NOT saying that you are being condemned or judged if you choose to or have to work outside the home. I am, however, celebrating the role of housewife, and homemaker; "the powerful role that shapes generations!" In this book, I want to encourage all women and men, that being a housewife is extremely important not only to our children, but to all of society. You may not agree with everything I say or how I suggest going about a particular task, not a problem. In all the years of going through military living quarters inspections I always passed. I want to share with you how I was able to achieve that. You may choose to be a little more relaxed in house cleaning, no worries. Whatever you do, please receive my thoughts from the heart of love for my fellow housewives.

I want to share with you some quotes of friends that I poled on this subject. Husbands and wives have given me their input and it is great!

"Stay-at-Home-Wives, what is your favorite thing about being a wife/mom?":

Anjelica Locke -"When my husband walks through the door and dinner is ready on the stove and there's a nice candle lit and the home is clean and I can just show him a bit of my appreciation for the hard work he does outside our home. Also being home with my children never worrying about if he's being harmed in a daycare environment!"

Cari Rogers - "My favorite thing about being a housewife is the thought that I'm so precious or important to my husband-that he cares for me so much-that I don't have to work. It's a gratitude born out of a "I can't believe I am this special" feeling.

My favorite thing about being a SAHM (Stay at Home Mom) is that I get to be with my kids. I adore each of my children. It is (mostly) me that influences what they watch, read and do. I am the one that gets to share life with them. It's like watching those first steps, but EVERYTHING is that cool. I teach them to read. I teach them to drive. I advise about relationships. I'm there for the telling of the job interview. I get to be there for the first everything. It's really a very special thing."

Nikki Westby Wiens - "Knowing that my man loves God enough to properly love me."

"Christian husbands of housewives, what is most important to you, or valuable in your mind, with regard to your wife being a homemaker and raising your children, rather than working full-time outside of the home? What is the one thing you most look forward to coming home at the end of the day? What ONE piece of advice would you give new housewives?"

Tommy - "I would rather we raise our children versus daycare. We are however, blessed financially that we were able for my wife to quit her job and raise our girls. Some people I know can't do that so I count my blessings over and over for it. I love coming home to a home cooked meal. I always ask my wife daily what I can do to help her, so her night can be easier. On days she has migraines, I cook, clean, etc. My favorite time is meal time with no TV, no phones, no interruptions. We all talk about our days and we pray together. Nothing gets better than that in my book."

David Parnell- "The most important thing to me is that the individual character each of my children is developing. Their posture of respect for the Lord is very noticeable. This is not natural and must be taught/trained. Additionally, their relationship(s) with one another is vastly different. The thing I look most forward to is a home full of warmth, acceptance, compassion, and I won't lie…a nice meal. My advice to new housewives is that with work and family, your husband may be caught between two vastly different worlds. Through your actions and feminine grace, remind him which "world" really loves him and respects him."

Jordan - "I like most that my wife can invest fully in the kids and me instead of things outside the home. She's not worn out on other things. I really enjoy coming to my wife and kids. We find the draw stronger of just wanting to be together. My advice to new housewives, use condoms! It's nice to have some just-the-two-of-you time before kiddos come."

I hope to show you what God's word says about the role of wife and mother. My goal and desire is to help you exchange society's lie for God's truth about our identities as women. I want to show ladies how fun, fulfilling and effective the role of housewife can be. We will get down to the very practical and very fun aspects of homemaking. We will discuss relationships with our husbands and our children and creative ways of supplementing the family income. Sit back, grab a cup, or a pot, of coffee and join me on this incredible journey of being "Just" a Housewife!

AS FOR ME AND MY HOUSE

Photo by: Ashlyn Gunter

Posted on our walls is the famous portion of scripture, Joshua 24:15, "…As for me and my house, we will serve the Lord."

The piece left out states, "And if it is evil in your eyes to serve the Lord, choose this day whom you will serve, whether the gods your fathers served in the region beyond the River, or the gods of the Amorites in whose land you dwell. But as for me and my house, we will serve the Lord." Joshua is telling the Israelites, "Look, you have to choose. You cannot serve two gods. Either you will serve the one true God, or you will serve false gods, period. There will be consequences. My house, will serve the Lord." As parents we are responsible for the way we run our house and raise our children. We are tasked for molding their hearts and minds after the Lord. Proverbs 22:6 tells us, "Start children off on the way they should go, and even when they are old they will not depart from it." Beginning from the womb our children are entrusted to us by God, and we can make a huge impact on how they live their lives.

Our children are our spiritual and physical responsibility. First Peter 5:2-3 says, "Be shepherds of God's flock that is under your care, watching over them - not because you must, but because you are willing, as God wants you to be; not pursuing dishonest gain, but eager to SERVE; [3] not lording it over those entrusted to you, but being EXAMPLES to the flock." (Emphasis added). Our children are not robots or slaves. We must show them honor and respect as fellow human beings.

I didn't always get this right. Let me tell you, my lack of honor and respect for my children as fellow humans produced rebellion and disrespect. It is our spiritual, godly duty to raise our children under the lordship of Jesus Christ. They must not only hear us speak of the Lord but they must see us live it day in and day out.

Our entire household should be run under the lordship of Jesus Christ. This includes marriage, children, finances, time management, homes, vehicles, entertainment, lawns…you name it…it all belongs to the Lord. When we see rightly, we live rightly. Homes should be alight with the glory of the Lord resting upon us as we serve and praise Him unashamedly. Our neighbors should have no doubt we are Christians; not because we brag about it, but because we live it. We are neighborly, helping those in need. We are kind, seek peace and respect others' property. We are not rude or annoying neighbors, but we are friendly and hospitable. We should be the light on the hill for all to see and run to. Not because we are special, but because Christ in us is holy.

We must remember that our children are a blessing, not a nuisance. Psalm 127:3-5, "Children are a heritage from the LORD, offspring a reward from him. [4] Like arrows in the hands of a warrior are children born in one's youth. [5] Blessed is the man whose quiver is full of them. They will not be put to shame when they contend with their opponents in court." Our children are a heritage FROM THE LORD. They are a gift from him. They are like arrows in the hands of a warrior, meaning that when handled rightly, they will have direction and victory. Blessed is the man whose quiver is full! Go, and multiply!

If we are going to have a household that serves that Lord we must know the biblical order of a godly home. The man is the head of the home, period. Bottom line. When the man, the husband, the father, is present in the family he is the head. He should lead the family spiritually. The man ought to guide the family in reading and studying the Bible and leading the family in daily prayers. The man is the final authority in the home. It is very difficult when a home does not start off this way, but it is possible to set things in right order with much love, grace and mercy from both the man and the woman. It is much easier to begin right though. Possibly said from personal experience.

Husbands, you have a very important role indeed and can set the course for how your children will live out their faith.

Ephesians 5:25-33 **Husbands, love** your **wives,** as Christ loved the church and <u>gave himself up for her</u>, [26] that he might sanctify her, having cleansed her by the washing of water **with the word** (The Bible), [27]so that he might present the church to himself in splendor, without spot or wrinkle or any such thing, that **she** might be holy and without blemish. [28] In the same way husbands should love their wives as their own bodies. He who loves his wife loves himself. [29] For no one ever hated his own flesh, but nourishes and cherishes it, just as Christ does the church, [30] because we are members of his body. [31] "Therefore a **man** shall leave his father and mother and hold fast to his **wife,** and the two shall become **one** flesh." [32] This mystery is profound, and I am saying that it refers to Christ and the church. [33] However, let each one of you **love his wife** as himself, and let the **wife** see that she **respects** her **husband**. (Emphasis added).

It is no mystery that women desire to be loved, cherished, and valued. Likewise, men desire to be respected and valued. When these two things are off kilter the entire household will feel the effects.

Back home our family has Friday dinner every week where the whole family comes together and eats dinner and spends time together. I miss participating in these family dinners since we live out of town. Our oldest daughter and her precious husband are such a sweet, young couple. I want to share something we can learn from our young married couple. At Friday dinners our daughter often arrives first, because her husband is finishing up his shift as a paramedic. As soon as her husband walks into the door she goes to him and they sit off by themselves and quietly talk alone, catching up on their day. They make each other a priority. I love that! We can learn so much from this. Husbands and wives must make each other a priority, even over the children…especially over the children. Our children need to see the proper order of family.

Titus Two shows us what a godly home looks like:

"But as for you, teach what accords with sound doctrine. ² Older men are to be sober-minded, dignified, self-controlled, sound in faith, in love, and in steadfastness. ³ Older women likewise are to be **reverent in behavior, not slanderers or slaves to much wine.** They are to **teach** what is good, ⁴ and so **train** the young women to **love their husbands and children,** ⁵ to be **self-controlled, pure, working at home, kind,** and **submissive to their own husbands,** that the word of God may not be reviled. ⁶ Likewise, urge the younger men to be self-controlled. ⁷ Show yourself in all respects to be a model of good works, and in your teaching show integrity, dignity, ⁸ and sound speech that cannot be condemned, so that an opponent may be put to shame, having nothing evil to say about us. ⁹ Bondservants are to be submissive to their own masters in everything; they are to be well-pleasing, not argumentative, ¹⁰ not pilfering, but showing all good faith, so that in everything they may adorn the doctrine of God our Savior.

¹¹ For the grace of God has appeared, bringing salvation for all people, ¹² training us to renounce ungodliness and worldly passions, and to live self-controlled, upright, and godly lives in the present age, ¹³ waiting for our blessed hope, the appearing of the glory of our great God and Savior Jesus Christ, ¹⁴ who gave himself for us to redeem us from all lawlessness and to purify for himself a people for his own possession who are zealous for good works.

¹⁵ Declare these things; exhort and rebuke with all authority. Let no one disregard you." (Emphasis added)

When our households serve the Lord and love, honor, and respect are found between the husband and wife, a godly home forms. As children enter the scene there will be no guessing as to how to rear them in an effective, biblical way. This household will be a smooth-running home that clearly serves the Lord. When visitors come in, they will have no doubt they have entered a godly home. Notice I did not highlight or emphasize the words to the men? Ladies, wives, our responsibility to respect and submit to our husbands is not dependent upon their actions or obedience to the Gospel. Whether they are obedient to Christ or not, we are still called to obedience in respecting and submitting to our husbands. The scriptures do not tell us to show him respect or submit to him when or if he is obedient. We are told to submit and show respect. Once I laid hold of this truth it changed everything! My obedience does not rely on my husband's obedience. Likewise, he is responsible for how he obeys the word of God. When both, the husband and the wife submit to the truth of the Gospel, our homes will be godly homes. Are there areas in your family that need readjustments leading you to fit into the godly profile of a home? Is Jesus the Lord of your house?

SERVING YOUR HUSBAND

Oh boy! Here we go. I'll just open with the elephant in the room. When we got married I was a fairly new Christian. I absolutely did not start off in my marriage being the biblical wife I was called to be. I somewhat did. However, I was full of pride, arrogance, rudeness, selfishness…okay, maybe I did not have a great beginning. Thankfully he is still my husband.

I did not have anyone discipling me and was trying to figure out this Christian walk on my own, which explains the many big failures. Some natural traits of mine aided me in being a wife and a homemaker. I probably learned some of these things from watching my mother and father and some were learned from my grandparents. I am of Sicilian and German descent and I believe Sicilian women were born to serve their husbands. When I was a little girl, I would pretend to be a housewife with children. Some of what I learned came from television (I do not recommend this!) Some came from Hollywood (I definitely do not recommend this!) Needless to say, I had some polishing to do on my role.

Since my childhood I couldn't wait to have a husband to cook for and create an inviting home for. These were things I believe I was naturally good at. The area I was not so good at was being a respectful and submissive wife. If I didn't agree with something I immediately made my opinion known and embarrassingly, may have acted like a child. I would nag my husband until I got my way. This is NOT the way to go about it, ladies. This goes against the word of God. I was functioning in rebellion to God and my husband. Is there any wonder our home was not as peaceful as it could have been? Proverbs 27:15-16 "A quarrelsome wife is like the dripping of a leaky roof in a rainstorm; [16] restraining her is like restraining the wind or grasping oil with the hand." Yikes! We do not want to be that wife!

Ladies, we were engineered to serve our Lord, our husbands, and others. God created us this way. Whenever you feel low about the position of servant, let me remind you of the greatest servant of all...Jesus

Christ. He selflessly served a wretched, sinning, rebellious people, giving his life on the cross at Calvary. He endured public shame and persecution. That is ultimate servant hood. Listen to this description of our Most High Servant, King Jesus:

Isaiah 53:4-7; 12 "Surely he has borne our griefs and carried our sorrows; yet we esteemed him stricken, smitten by God, and afflicted. [5] But **he** was pierced for **our** transgressions; **he** was crushed for **our** iniquities; upon **him** was the chastisement that brought **us** peace, and with **his** wounds **we** are healed. [6] All we like sheep have gone astray; we have turned - every one - to his own way; and the Lord has laid on **him** the iniquity of **us** all. [7] **He** was oppressed, and **he** was afflicted, yet he **opened not** his mouth; like a lamb that is led to the slaughter, and like a sheep that before its shearers is **silent**, so he **opened not** his mouth."

[12] "Therefore I will divide him a portion with the many, and he shall divide the spoil with the strong, because **he** poured his soul to death and was numbered with the transgressors; yet **he** bore the sin of many, and m**akes intercession** for the **transgressors**." (Emphasis added)

If Christ Jesus our Lord is the perfect example of servant hood and we are to model ourselves after him, might we consider the importance of servant hood, especially to our husbands? While Jesus was laying down his life for the sinner he did not once open his mouth to defend himself or to complain about his position of servant.

We were created to serve our husbands with respect, love, and sincerity. Ephesians 5:33 says, "However, each one of you also must love his wife as he loves himself, and the **wife** must **respect** her **husband**." Notice this verse doesn't say, "When he loves you," or "When he is nice to you," or "When you get your way." It just says, "Respect your husband."

In working in ministry with other ladies, they often tell me they will show respect to their husband when he starts treating them with love and respect. That is not biblical and is in rebellion to the command of the Father. It is not up to us to decide when we obey the Lord and when we do not. Either he is Lord, or we are making ourselves Lord. If we truly see him as Lord, then we will respect our husbands regardless of his actions. This is an area I am still growing in and I believe we all can. This is especially true if you were not raised in a godly home where biblical submission was not practiced and honored. There are times when the flesh creeps in. We must allow the Spirit of God to reign in our hearts, quashing the flesh. (There are times where there is physical or emotional abuse taking place, this is not what I am referring to. If either of these are occurring I strongly encourage you to seek Christian counseling and help.)

Let's get practical. What does serving our husband look like? We will start with the natural order of the day. Know your husband. Does he prefer to eat breakfast in the morning or have coffee? My husband has not always been a big breakfast eater. He does enjoy his coffee though. Some days if he has enough time he will sit down and enjoy breakfast. Either way, make it a point to get up in the morning and prepare his coffee and/or his breakfast. I was not always good about this, especially when our children were babies. Our oldest daughter is nine years older than our next child. Then we had three practically right in a row. I took advantage of sleeping whenever I could. However, because we were a military family my husband was often deployed or away at training, so when he was home, I tried to make it a point to serve him more diligently. Plus, he enjoyed spending time with the children so I could cook breakfast. I am still not always good about this but am making more of an effort to wake-up early and cook breakfast for him. This shows our husbands that we not only appreciate them but we are willing to make a small sacrifice to invest in them as they make a huge sacrifice going to work each day.

You want a positive, healthy start to the day. Always kiss each other good-bye, you never know if that will be your last encounter with him, or any of your family for that matter. When you leave a loved one, always tell them you love them no matter the prior conversation. I know too many people who suffered the unexpected loss of a loved one and did not exchange loving words for their last conversation. You do not want that hanging over you. Send your husband off with some baked goodies for work, or a prepared lunch. Let him know how much you appreciate all he does for you and your family. Tell him how much you appreciate him as he walks out the door. Maybe tell him how handsome he is and how you cannot wait to see him later that day. Whatever you do, do not nag him about something he hasn't done or that you want done. Let him leave the house peacefully. You want him to want to come home. There is a time to bring your needs and concerns with your husband, but that time is NOT when he is walking out the door or coming home from work. Wait until he has come home, settled in, and had time to decompress. Ask him how his day was. If he doesn't want to talk about it, forget it, let it go. You don't need to know everything that happened. He will appreciate this. When he is ready, he will share what's on his mind.

Use the time your husband is at work as an opportunity to serve him. Make that house his castle! Make sure when he comes, he can walk into a peaceful, organized and comfortable home. The last thing you want is for your husband to return to chaos and disorganization. Make the beds. Pick up the clutter. Wash the dishes, etc. Show him how much you appreciate what he does by caring for and maintaining a pleasant home. I'll get more into how you can incorporate your children into this model in the "Childrearing" chapters.

While he is at work, do your best not to nag him through text messages or phone calls with complaints or a to-do list. If you are going to text or call him, make sure it is to encourage him or send him a flirty message. Keep it short. Let him know you trust him and respect his time and hard work. I speak on this subject from personal experience. If it is at all possible hold your questions or needs until after he has come home and had a chance to relax.

Make every effort to have a hot meal ready for your husband when he returns home. If you have younger children and more than two, I get it, you may not always be able to prepare a home cooked meal. You can, however, at least have a hot meal ready for him. This is a great time to train your children that they are not the priority in the home. Take advantage of jarred pasta sauces and Italian sausage, pasta and ready-made salads. This is a healthy meal that is quick and simple. Not to mention, you can repurpose those lovely jars for drinking glasses (which come with amazing lids to prevent spills) and they make great leftover containers you can safely microwave. It is also helpful to prepare larger meals that you can stretch over several days or freeze. Soups, stews, spaghetti, lasagna, and casseroles are great for this.

When your husband walks through that door after work greet him with positive attention. Love on him. Let the children love on him. Ask him if he needs anything and let him know dinner will be ready when he is. Dinnertime is a very special time for the family and should be protected. While it may not be feasible every single night, do it as often as possible. Or, do it for breakfast or lunch. Sit down at a set table together without the television on or electronic devices available. This is a perfect opportunity to train the children in chores and participating in household responsibilities. The moment your husband walks through the door is not the time to tell him how terrible your day was or how awful the children behaved, unless you are looking to start a fight or create a negative atmosphere.

Set some time aside for you and your husband to participate in a hobby together. Find something the two of you can do together, without the children. If you are like us and lived away from family, find trusted church friends to take care of your children while you go out. If that is not possible make time after their bedtime. My husband and I often enjoy going out to nice restaurants and a clean movie (Which is getting harder to come by, although Christian producers are beginning to put out some amazing products.) While he was still active-duty when he was home, we would play golf (I really just had fun driving the golf cart around). We have always enjoyed having friends over to play games and hang out. Spending time as a couple with older, more mature, godly couples helps you learn what a healthy marriage looks like and see that they do exist.

Though being a housewife is very rewarding, it comes with a lot of responsibilities. A housewife does not get to sit around all day and watch television or talk to her best friend on the phone. No sister, being a housewife is a big job and is not for the faint of heart. In later chapters I will discuss in detail what your day to day responsibilities look like. I want you to grasp that being a housewife is one of the most important roles you will ever hold. You will be holding the fort down while your husband goes out and earns the money to provide for you and your family. He puts a lot of trust in you to run the home well. The Lord is entrusting you to serve your husband and raise your children in a godly way.

Deuteronomy 6 tells us, [5] You shall love the Lord your God with all your heart and with all your soul and with all your might. [6] And these words that I command you today shall be on your heart. ⁷ **You** shall **teach** them **diligently to your children**, and shall **talk of them** when you **sit** in your house, and when you **walk by the way** (When you drive nowadays), and when you **lie down**, and when you **rise**. ⁸ You shall bind them as a sign on your hand, and they shall be frontlets between your eyes. ⁹ You shall write them on the doorposts of your house and on your gates. (Emphasis added)

The word of the Lord should be very present in your home. You should be teaching your children the word of God and the history of his people. Your husband should be leading in this as well. If you happen to be married to a husband who is not doing this, that does not mean you can't or shouldn't. You absolutely should! Pray that your husband will desire to join you and eventually lead in this area. Your children need to see you set aside personal time to be in the word and in prayer. They need to see you doing that just as the apostles saw Jesus doing that. This may not sound like serving your husband. Let me tell you, the way you raise your children shows how you serve your husband. You want to represent him well.

Another way you can serve your husband is by managing finances responsibly. I have not always done this well either. Much of what I share, I share from personal experience and failure. Bless the Lord, he has shown me the better way. I am growing each day. This is another reason I find home schooling to be such a blessing. I never really learned about managing finances in school. With home schooling you decide what your children will learn. We have taught our children from an early age that it is important to manage money in a godly way and we have let them learn within the safety of our guidance. This too, serves your husband in that how your children turn out as adults reflects on him. I know, they seem to get all the credit publicly, but it is widely known that the mother plays a huge role in the upbringing of their children. It is not important who gets the credit. By the way, remember that as a married couple you are one. So, when he gets credit for how the children turned out, that means you do too! You are a team. Your husband is not and should never be your competition (Unless you're playing Monopoly, then he is absolutely your competition!)

We serve our husbands in our honor and devotion to them. Romans 12:10 teaches, "Love one another with brotherly affection. **Outdo** one another in showing honor." (Emphasis added) Let us not take our husbands for granted. Not only our words, but our actions should show how much we appreciate them. Give him back rubs, foot massages, his favorite dessert, etc. Find ways to show him honor and love. Wash his car inside and out. Make sure his clothes are clean and freshly pressed, if necessary for his work. Make sure his underwear is not tattered and his socks don't have holes. I challenge you to go about your day seeking ways to honor and serve him.

Always speak highly of him to others. Never put your husband down in front of anyone, especially your children. Ashamedly, I can tell you from experience this will hurt your marriage. It does not matter what is going on, do all that you can to protect his reputation and character.

We have experienced some pretty difficult things in our marriage. Putting your husband down in front of others will only make things worse and create a major lack of trust between you. He will lose respect for you and thus lose the desire to make amends. Remember, men yearn for respect. Putting your husband down is the opposite of respect. This will crush a marriage faster than anything else. If you must speak to someone about struggles in your marriage, make sure it is a trusted friend or family member, and that it is done in love and respect, not to win someone's support for your side. There are no sides in a marriage. You and he are ONE. If he fails, you fail. If he hurts, you hurt. HE is NOT your enemy! Never forget that. Your heart should always seek peace and reconciliation. Stay away from any action that doesn't promote harmony.

If you run into a problem with your marriage, I highly recommend Christian counseling, as opposed to venting to your friends. Be especially cautious of how you speak about your husband to family, both yours and his. Your words should never be the reason someone loses respect for him.

Do what you can to serve your man! Make him feel like a king in his home. Celebrate him. Speak highly of him to your children.

Be open and honest with your husband, at the right time. If you feel like you are not receiving enough love, attention, or affection from him, let him know. Do not do this in an accusatory manner, but from a heart posture of love and sincerity. Wait to bring this up when he is not at work or just walking in the door. Also, before bringing him your concerns, go to the Lord in prayer and ask Holy Spirit if there is anything you need to change. Is there something you have done to cause his actions? Be completely honest and very concise. Men are people of few words and desire to hear few words. They would prefer that we get right to the point. We do not need to paint this, long, drawn-out story just to say, "I feel like we aren't spending as much time together."

Stay away from saying things such as, "You always… or you never…" For example, "You never say, 'I love you' when we're in public." (This is just a random example.) What you are saying is that you are keeping score of his failures. This is not the message we want to send, regardless if he does this very thing. Christ has never done this to us and we should not be doing it to our husbands or anyone else.

Once you have worked an issue out, never bring it up again, especially during a disagreement that has absolutely nothing to do with that incident. Again, what you are conveying is that even though you worked that issue out you haven't really forgiven him and continue to hold it against him. Christ does not continually bring up our past mistakes. In fact, that is a tool of the Accuser, Satan. We do not want to use Satan's tactics do we?

In serving our husbands it is wise to learn his love language. What does he respond to most and how does he prefer to show and be shown love? If words of affirmation stimulate him, make it a point to speak words of affirmation to him often. Make sure your words to him are genuine; otherwise it could be received as patronizing, or belittling. If he loves to give gifts, then show him how much you appreciate the gift by not stuffing it in your drawer but wearing it when you go out. Learn to speak to his heart. Perhaps he really enjoys great meals or desserts. Even if this is not your strong suit, learn to prepare great meals and desserts. Remember though, learning to speak his love language is not the same thing as manipulation. Your goal is not to manipulate him into doing or giving what you want. The goal is serving your husband with love and genuine intention.

Finally, let us pray. I greatly encourage you to pray for your husband often, always, constantly. Pray for him while he sleeps. Pray for him as he walks out the door. Pray for him while he is at work. Pray for him before you are married, before you have even met him! (Our daughter did this, and our other children pray for their future bride or groom.) Pray for him while he isn't with you. Here is an example:

"Father, I cover my dear husband in prayer right now as he is on his way to work. I thank you for guarding him and protecting him as he drives, from mechanical problems, deer, and other drivers. Keep him alert and focused on the road. I thank you that he is your son, an heir to your kingdom. I thank you that he is covered by the living blood of Jesus and that everything he touches will prosper because of the divine favor that rests upon him. I thank you that he is highly favored in the work place and that others see him as a beacon of light and a model for everything that is good and respectable. I thank you that your wisdom guides him, that Holy Spirit reveals all truth to him. I thank you that he seeks your counsel before making decisions. I thank you that his relationships at work are godly, pure, and profitable. I thank you that he is highly regarded, respected and sought after. I thank you that he is at peace knowing that I am running our home according to your standards and that there is no reason for distraction from his work. I thank you for protecting him while he is at work, for keeping him healthy. I thank you for bringing him home safely at the end of the day and blessing our time together as a family. In your mighty, powerful, precious name I pray these things over my husband, your son, amen!"

One thing that has really helped me in my later years is seeing my husband rightly. He is first and foremost a son of the High Priest, the Creator of all things, the Lord of lords and the King of kings. Secondly, he is my beloved husband, my best-friend. He is NEVER my enemy. When I see my husband as a son of God I see him through the lens of grace and mercy. I see him redeemed, standing as a righteous, pure and holy son and heir of the kingdom of God. This helps me to respond to him with a right and pure heart rather than a defensive or condemning heart. Let us remember, there is only one Judge, and we are not Him.

First Peter 3:1-2 says, "Likewise, wives, be subject to your own husbands, so that even if some do not obey the word, they may be won without a word by the conduct of their wives, ² when they see your respectful and pure conduct."

So even if your husband is not a believer, it is possible to win him over to the Lord simply by your respectfulness to him and your conduct, which consists of love, grace, mercy and forgiveness. Also in First Peter, 4:8, "Above all, keep loving one another earnestly, since love covers a multitude of sins." Even if your husband doesn't know how to act rightly according to God's word, your love carries forgiveness when he wrongs you. If he is an unbeliever or a spiritually immature Christian, chances are likely he doesn't even know the right way to behave. But by your love, conduct and respect for him, you can win him over to the Lord. I can promise you one thing for certain, nit-picking, criticizing, and arguing with him will do the exact opposite. Love earnestly.

I vividly recall a time when we were struggling through some major setbacks. My husband was overseas in Afghanistan and I was doing the dutiful thing of praying for my husband. It went something like this…"Lord, please show him his errors. Show him that he needs to fix such and such. Show him how he has hurt me. Give him a heart for me. Show him how to love me." Wow…really? How arrogant of me! But it was in that moment, as I knelt on my bedroom floor with the sun's hot rays beaming on my back, the Lord spoke to my heart. Bless the Lord. He is so gracious and merciful. He said, "My dear daughter, who are you to tell me how to fix MY son? You keep praying for him but pray like this…'Father, I ask you to bless my husband in all that he does. I pray for your favor to be upon him. I pray that you would show me how to love him, show me how to serve him. I pray that he would have a fresh revelation of you and a personal encounter with you, that you would be made more real to him than ever before. I ask that you would bless our marriage and bring healing and reconciliation. If there is anything in my heart that needs to be changed please show me. Help me to be the wife that my husband needs right now. Lord, please show me how to love him as your son and not my enemy. Help me to love him rightly. Amen.'"

Let us pray for our husbands always. This is the greatest gift we could ever give them.

PROVERBS 31 WIFE
EARNING SUPPLEMENTAL INCOME FROM HOME

Oh, let me count the ways I have earned income from home because there were times we were in tight spots financially. While I didn't necessarily need to go to work full-time, I needed to do something to help offset our financial dry spell. Please know that no matter your background or degree, there is always something you can do to earn income, either from home or part-time, while someone you trust stays with your children. You have a skill or talent that can be used to earn income, especially in this day and age. There is no reason why you cannot earn some extra money.

While my husband served in the military I was quite politically involved and did investigative research work in the fields of counter-terrorism and counter-intelligence. Being heavily involved in our local politics, this created a major networking capability for me. I was paid to speak at various engagements and conduct seminars on matters I was familiar with. I wrote a blog and earned money from the ads that ran on my page. I wrote articles for other blogs and newspapers and received compensation. I actually wrote a few political speeches and got paid for that! There were even times I was paid to do investigative research on a particular subject/person. Writing is a skill I've always been passionate about and seem to be somewhat good at. I capitalized this niche and put it to work. For a while I made money-building websites for people.

While we were on the east coast with the military, I taught aerobics and fitness classes at the gym. Since I am a nationally certified personal trainer, I got paid to teach. Several people I met through politics or church hired me to train them. These are things that did not require me to be away from home for long periods of time and was able to set my own schedule.

While we lived in Texas on our small ranch, we raised a LOT of chickens (I think we had over 75 at one point). We raised free-range, pastured chickens. These were highly sought after eggs. We sold our eggs locally for $4.00 a dozen! There was always a long waiting list of customers. We sold turkeys and sheep for meat. The children helped out by making sea salt scrubs to sell on our website. We monetized our property and home as best we could. How can you use your property for income? You can take care of other children in your home; sell baked goods, crafts, clothes, etc. I know several ladies who sell clothing lines or jewelry from their home and are quite successful with it.

If you are crafty, your window to the money-making world just opened even more. I have several friends who will buy really cheap, used furniture at second-hand stores or antique shops and they refinish them or paint them with creative designs. They make decent money doing this. Some of them make wall art, floral arrangements, wreaths, and all types of home decor. A few of my friends are doing well making pottery pieces, dinnerware, and cookware. The young lady who did the art for my book, *Love to Reconcile*, is selling her art on Etsy.

I currently am a companion sitter for a hospice company. My hours are very sparse, and I like it that way. I choose whether to accept or deny offered hours. When a patient goes imminent (has less than 72 hours projected to live) they call in companion sitters. A companion sitter is someone who literally sits with a dying patient so they are not alone in their last hours of life. We do absolutely no medical care. I can read and write or pray and talk with the patient. Mind you, at this point, most of the patients are not coherent enough to communicate. Sometimes family members visit. We either stay in the room with them or sit in the lobby. This is part of the job. Our drive to and from the nursing home is calculated as hours, and we get compensated for gas. If you can handle being present when a patient dies you may look into this opportunity in your area. Not every nursing home pays companion sitters, many only use volunteers.

Another hobby of mine is cooking, so I would turn to it for income. I did not invest much in advertising, rather word of mouth. I wasn't interested in getting inundated with orders, just making extra money to help us get by while raising our children and taking care of our home. Word got out quickly. On a few occasions I set-up a business page on Facebook to handle orders and show what I offered. Running a Facebook page is free versus building a website. This is usually enough to run such a business.

More recently, I got a part-time job with Instacart. Instacart is a company that hires people to grocery shop for customers. You need a reliable, insured vehicle. You may need additional insurance to cover commercial use. The application processes is simple and you are working within seven business days. Because I grocery shop a lot, I figured I'd be good at this. It is such an easy job and again, I make my own schedule. I am still employed by Instacart and can accept hours at any time. The only thing with this type of job is you have to make sure that the demand in your area is worth it. The demand is not nearly as high where I live now as it was in Dallas, TX. In Dallas the demand was so high that bonuses and extra hours were offered.

Similar jobs consist of DoorDash and Uber. I am employed with Uber but never started driving, mainly because I don't feel comfortable driving in the city near me. It is best if your husband is ok with you doing this type of job, since you will have strangers in your vehicle.

That's one of the advantages to Instacart and DoorDash, you aren't transporting people, you are only putting food in your car and then delivering to the customer. You decide what areas you work in. The safety protocols are great for these companies. On one of my grocery runs with Instacart, I got a little lost. It didn't take long for an Instacart agent to call and check on me. They are always aware of your location. Another thing you want to take into consideration is the distance from each job. If you pick-up groceries in one area and then accept a run in an area over thirty minutes away you are not only using your fuel for that trip but you are losing time paid. You are not paid for the time spent driving; you are simply paid per order completed. However, the tips can often be amazing! This is where a good attitude and people skills come in. Make sure you have a good cell phone carrier. Once inside the grocery store reception can be challenging for some carriers. It can be very frustrating if the app won't work, because your signal continually gets dropped.

Hear me friend-you have skills! You are good at something! If you have a home, a car, a driver's license, a kitchen, a sewing machine, a camera, a phone, etc. you can earn money! Use technology to your advantage and learn a skill that will earn money. Can you walk a dog? Repair computers? Take great pictures? The possibilities are endless. It may not always be necessary to earn extra money. But when it is, the sky is the limit. Before falling into a state of panic, take a step back and evaluate all the ways and means with which you can earn money. Get creative. Think outside the box. Go after it!

CREATIVELY CUTTING COSTS

One of the first things to do when finances get tight is find ways to cut spending. Often, this will be all it takes to alleviate the pressure. Just like the endless possibilities in creating supplemental income, there are endless possibilities in cutting spending.

First, sit down with your husband and decide what are the necessities versus extras in your life. Once you establish this, begin paring away. You may not necessarily begin with the most expensive item rather, the easiest thing to give-up. I would not suggest removing something that will cause even more stress in your family or removing something that is good for your family, such as a gym membership. This can bring added stress to an already difficult season.

So you have made your list of necessities and extras. Great! Now, begin going through these lists with your husband and possibly your children. One of the best ways to cut costs is by being a conscientious grocery shopper. Stay away from the inner aisles in the store. This is where the trap items are, such as comfort foods and processed foods. They're usually more expensive too. Focus on the outer aisles and the produce section, they are much safer. Look at store brand items. We have bought store brand items for a very long time for most products. There isn't much of a difference. But with some items, you'll want name brand. Organic items are more available, even from store brands. Start using coupons and pay attention to sales. Make more of your food at home instead of buying pre-made meals. This is a great time to begin eating healthier as a family. The grocery store is a great start to cutting your bills.

Next, consider how often and where you dine out. Perhaps cut this back to once a month and make it a special occasion. Have your family get dressed-up and choose a reasonably priced restaurant. Let your children get dessert, if it fits in the budget. If not, get ice cream and make sundaes at home. If dining out is too much, then spend a little extra for some steaks from the store and make a very special meal. You can still dress nicely for it and turn it into a special occasion. Play board games as a family afterward. Also, more restaurants are participating in GroupOn deals or if you check-in on social media, they will give you a discount. (Just remember the security ramifications of posting your whereabouts publicly).

Other areas you can evaluate include clothes shopping. If you stop and consider how often you wear what is in your closet, I have a feeling you will realize you seldom wear a majority of what is in there. We tend to gravitate toward about ten outfits. If you find this to be true, this is a great time to go through your closet and sell the clothes you seldom wear. Have a garage sale! Also, shopping at second-hand stores is a great way to limit spending. Many stores will give you a credit in return for clothes that you give. If your clothes are getting holes, mend them rather than replace them. Our children learned at a young age that tears in clothes can easily be sewn or patched. We have become a "replace" society. As soon as something is broken, we run out to buy a new one. This isn't always necessary. In fact, it seldom is.

This is a good time to discuss home and vehicle maintenance, rather than paying someone else to do what you can easily do at home. If I need to, I can change the oil in our vehicles. I can change a tire. I have learned how to replace the components in the tank of our toilets and made small repairs on our washer. Our youngest daughter has repaired our weed eaters, multiple times. Learning how to do these things can alleviate a lot of major expenses. By the way, taking care of our appliances, vehicles, etc. will help a great deal in avoiding major repairs. Regularly scheduled maintenance will extend the life of your appliances and vehicles. We want to be good stewards of what the Lord has blessed us with.

Another area to cut spending is entertainment. This might include video games, movies, subscriptions, sports, etc. Going to the movies is a lot more expensive than renting one. Cable and satellite is becoming outdated. We personally quit subscribing to satellite television over nine years ago. We saved over $2,000 a year! Then, we sold all of our televisions sets (three). This also cut on our energy costs. We began using our laptop to watch DVD's or online viewing. Just recently we subscribed to online streaming instead of satellite.

Usually these subscriptions are around $10 a month rather than $120. You may want to limit how many you subscribe to. Evaluate your hobbies and decide if they're really necessary.

Other areas to consider include your home's energy and water consumption. Limit your shower times, use cold water to wash clothes instead of hot. Use the dishwasher versus hand washing. Turn the air conditioner to 72° in the hot seasons and the heater to 68° in the cold months. If you can handle it, we would actually set our heater at 62° and our air conditioner at 82°. We use the fireplace and fans to compensate and dress to fit our personal comfort level. This is doable. You just have to be willing to give up a little. Your body accommodates pretty quickly.

Another way you can cut costs is planning out your trips for all your needs. Instead of making multiple trips to the grocery each week, plan your meals ahead of time and go once. Since you know you're going to be out, plan other errands and go in the order that will use the least amount of fuel instead of popping back and forth across town. Talk with neighbors and see about coordinating grocery store runs. While in the military, we did this a lot and we took turns driving each week.

A fun way to cut costs is by finding a dual purpose in your purchases. For example, when we buy jars of salsa or pasta sauce, we buy the brand that has jars that can be used as drinking glasses or food storage containers. We have a ton of mason jar glasses from doing this very thing. If one gets broken it is not a big deal, it was $2.37 and we have tons of them! By the way, these can be used for crafts such as vases, money saving jars, good behavior jars, holiday decorations and whatever else you can think of. Start looking at how your consumable purchases can be repurposed. Plastic ice cream tubs make for good large food storage containers. You can use paper towel and toilet paper rolls for art projects, holiday decorations, fire starters and math manipulatives. If you keep all of your dryer lint and wad it up into small balls and then place it inside the toilet paper tubes, these make great fire starters for the family campfire.

When you cook, think about how you can turn that large meal into a variety of leftovers. The large leftover turkey can be made into turkey sandwiches and turkey tortilla soup (see recipes in the *Favorite Recipes* chapter). Prepare larger meals you can stretch over a few days and your husband can take to work, so he doesn't have to eat out. Prepare on-the-go meals for you and the children instead of buying pre-made meals.

Ask the Lord to show you creative ways to cut costs and discover supplemental sources of income. Think more objectively and outside the box. Making your own Christmas ornaments is a lot cheaper and a lot of fun. Include the children and create lasting memories. Just because money is tight doesn't mean life has to be miserable. There are so many creative ways to spend less money. This is only a season, and you will get through it. Philippians 4:4-7 tells us, "Rejoice in the Lord always; again I will say, rejoice. [5] Let your reasonableness be known to everyone. The Lord is at hand; [6] do not be anxious about anything, but in everything by prayer and supplication with thanksgiving let your requests be made known to God. [7] And the peace of God, which surpasses all understanding, will guard your hearts and your minds in Christ Jesus."

RAISING DISCIPLES

Parenting is such a blessing from the Lord. Psalm 127:3 "Behold, children are a heritage from the Lord, the fruit of the womb a reward."

Children are simply little people. They are not to be despised or talked down to. Children deserve the same respect adults do.

When raising children, we should treat them as small people. Their minds are just as precious as the adult mind. When speaking to children, be cautious of using "baby talk." Instead, speak to them as we speak to adults. It's okay to use smaller words, but don't speak in a baby voice. This is very important for their developmental growth.

Children are more capable of handling situations than we give them credit for. Sure, there are going to be things they don't need to know, such as the details of your finances or your bills. Be cautious of telling your children that you can't afford this and that. However, they should be taught how to handle finances and the money that the Lord entrusts to them. So, show them that flippantly spending money isn't always prudent. Show them the importance of tithing, saving, and investing. We created jars or envelopes with these three categories and helped our children learn how to manage their money. They are capable of doing this as early as three years old. When our children were around four or five years old, I helped them make small purchases at the store. This included teaching them how to communicate with the cashier. I taught them the importance of looking someone in the eye when speaking to them. They also learned the importance of math in everyday life.

As far as allowances go we made it clear that their regular, daily chores were expected to be completed before they could earn money for doing extra chores. They learned that there are things they are expected to do without compensation. Maintaining their room is an expected chore. They should also clean up after themselves, period. If they get something out, they put it away. This can and should be taught from the time they are mobile. It will take a lot of repeating but is well worth it. They are not incapable of learning expected or appropriate behavior. I highly recommend the *Love and Logic* parenting materials found in the "Recommended Resources" list at the back of this book.

Back to the concept that children can handle more than we give them credit for. I suggest not hiding difficult subjects from them. Death would be one of those subjects. You may not want to go into great detail about a particular subject, but hiding things from children can do more harm than good, because they are not prepared to handle difficult situations when they arise.

When my husband was still active duty, we were very open with our children. We would speak with them as soon as we received word of his next deployment and prepared them for the fact that he would be leaving soon to go to another country and to fight the bad guys. We explained the very real possibilities of what could happen and teach them how to pray for him before he left and while he was gone. We never lied to them or told them he was just going on a trip. If something bad happened to him, can you imagine the shock and betrayal they would feel if we hadn't told them? I knew parents who would tell their children daddy was on a plane. Every time a plane flew over, they thought it was daddy coming home. That is not fair to the children. If we prepare our children for difficult situations, they are less likely to respond with fear and anxiety. They are also more likely to trust us more. This is very important, especially as they grow older. You want your children to trust you.

Creating trust between you and your children is crucial. That bond should be created early on. As a military family, one of the most important things for our children was letting them know that we are there for them and we are a safe place. If they woke up during the night and were scared, wanting to stay in bed with us we let them. I know, we broke the rule of co-sleeping with our children. Because we were a military family and daddy was often deployed in "Hot Zones," we felt it especially important to build this bond. We wanted to create an environment where they felt safe and protected. You may disagree with this, and that is perfectly fine. I will say that our children have always known they could come to us with anything at any time. They felt safe. You have enough wisdom to know if they are taking advantage of this or if they are truly frightened. We don't want our children feeling scared in their own home.

Another way to build trust with your children is to exhibit consistency in your training. If touching the stove is prohibited today, then it should be prohibited tomorrow. If they are not allowed to watch a particular show in the morning, they shouldn't be permitted to watch it later on that day. This type of inconsistency is not only confusing to the child, but it can build a lack of trust. If you tell your child not to throw their toy again or you will spank them, follow through if they throw it again. This is a great time to learn how to match discipline with the misbehavior. If your child doesn't know something is not allowed they shouldn't be disciplined for it. Use this opportunity to teach them.

The next time they break the rule, begin discipline. As soon as children are mobile, they are capable of discerning right from wrong. It takes consistency and much perseverance. Yet another reason it is good for them to be raised in the home under your rules in their early years to avoid confusion.

Set a few simple rules that are easy to understand. Do not over-inundate young children with too many rules and rules that are beyond their comprehension. That is not fair to the child and sets them up for failure. It also sets you up for major frustration. When you ask them to do something give them one simple task at a time. For example: "Suzie, take your blanket to your bed right now please." This is much more effective than this, "Suzie, take your blanket, doll, brush and coloring books and put them in your toy chest and your blanket on your bed." When Suzie returns from putting her blanket on her bed then you can have her put her brush in the bathroom. Then, she can put her coloring books in her toy chest. Do you see how this works? Simple is better. It may take her a little longer, but this will eliminate frustration and undue discipline. As stated in a previous chapter it is important teach children early on that when they are done with something, they should put it back where it belongs before getting something else out. This eliminates clutter and teaches responsibility.

When it comes to potentially dangerous situations one word, simple commands are best. If your child is running towards the street you want to speak sternly, "STOP." If they are reaching for the stovetop, "STOP." You are not necessarily yelling at them but speaking with a stern voice communicates urgency and seriousness. After they are safe, explain why they are not to do whatever it was they were engaging in. Some parents count to three, giving their children a window of time to obey. But when you tell your child to do something, they need to comply right away. Counting communicates the message that you were not serious the first time. It also creates confusion. If you tell them to put their toy in their room and they hear you and do not obey, they need to be disciplined immediately for their disobedience. If you wait too long, they will not associate the discipline with the misbehavior. Not only will it confuse them, it can breed distrust and bitterness toward you. If your child is a toddler and doesn't obey right away, a simple time out, or taking that toy away and placing it somewhere they can still see it but not access it can be very effective. This may sound cruel, but it is a reminder that if they want the toy, they need to be responsible for it. If you place it out of sight, they forget about it. I would typically take things away for a few hours or a day when they were toddlers. As they got older, the length of time would increase. This is true for any discipline. As the child grows older, their discipline will increase according to what they can handle emotionally and mentally. We are training our little ones to become grown adults. This begins from the time they are mobile.

Reading to your child from the time they are in the womb is a wonderful way to bond with them. It also stimulates their growing brain. Get animated with your reading, make it fun! Point to the dog and sound out the word, "Dog." Point to colors and tell them what they are. Read a sentence of a familiar book and begin leaving a word out and letting them say it. For example: "The moon will come out and soon it will be…?" Read the end of the sentence as a question and wait for your child to respond with, "Night." This helps their brain make the connection of seeing, hearing and saying. Believe it or not, children can begin learning to read at age three. Our youngest child was reading well by the time she was four years old. Talk through the ABC's and numbers every single day with them. Place the letter and number magnets on the refrigerator. Make learning toys and books readily available. I encourage you to greatly limit electronic toys, especially in the early years.

Another area that could easily fit in the "Family Health" chapter is that of entertainment and what our children's little eyes see and ears hear. I did a video lesson on this very subject with a focus on video games; but the gist of the study can be applied to all forms of entertainment. The video lesson can be viewed at the ministry Facebook page - *Damascus Report,* or: **https://www.damascusreport.com/post/entertainment_safeornot**

The things our children see and hear have more of an effect on them than we may realize. I shared in the "Family Health" chapter about my personal experiences while visiting friends' homes. The things that were on their televisions and the activities that were allowed to happen affected me in a serious way for years to come. I was exposed to sexually illicit movies, drug use, and teenagers and young adults participating in semi-sexual activity. We cannot completely protect our children one hundred percent of the time, but when we are able, we have an obligation to.

The idea that we should expose our children to the world because they'll eventually be living in it on their own is not a biblical concept. Proverbs 22:6 "Train up a child in the way he should go; even when he is old he will not depart from it." Even further, Matthew 18:5-6, "Whoever receives one such child in my name receives me, 6 but whoever causes one of these little ones who believe in me to sin, it would be better for him to have a great millstone fastened around his neck and to be drowned in the depth of the sea." (This was Jesus talking.) This is pretty clear. If we expose our children intentionally to sinful behavior for the sake of training them how to handle it, we are exposing them unnecessarily to darkness.

Bankers are trained in knowing very well the genuine thing. They are exposed to the true money over and over. They know it so well; they will recognize a counterfeit when they come across it. They are not exposed to the counterfeit repeatedly to be able to recognize it. The true is same for our spiritual walk. We must know the truth of the Light in order to recognize the darkness. As parents, we are obligated to train our children in the right way, not the wrong way. We repeatedly expose them to the right way and when they happen to come across the wrong way, they will easily recognize it as a counterfeit, a way that is not in agreement with the Gospel.

There are so many opportunities for our children to be exposed to evil by way of television, video games, and social media. It is our job to protect them and give them godly counsel. We want to be cautious of exposing our children to things they are not yet ready for. Social media can be used for the glory of the Kingdom. It can also very easily be used for wickedness. In fact, many child predators use social media to lure children into their hands. A five-year- old is not mature enough for social media. A thirteen-year-old is most likely not ready for social media. In fact, most sixteen-year-olds will not be in a position to handle social media with wisdom and experience. If you choose to allow your children to be on social media, I strongly recommend that you not only have access to their accounts, but that you regularly monitor their activity, especially private messages, photos, and friend requests. Know their logins and passwords. The same goes for their cell phones, laptops, and any other devices with Internet access.

Regarding the internet, heavily monitor this constantly. Take advantage of the resources available to lock down your Internet to protect them from accidentally or intentionally accessing illicit sites. If you belong to Home School Legal Defense Association I believe you have discounts to many of these tools. Don't allow your children on the Internet behind closed doors. While they're using the internet, have them in a common area in your home where you can keep an eye on their activity. This is actually a good habit for all family members to abide by, including mom and dad.

Back to the video game issue. Video games bring up several concerns. First of all, they can become addictive very quickly. They are a time-sucker. Before you know it you've played for three hours. Also, the ads on video games, even children's games or innocent word games, can be very explicit. On a simple word game they were running ads that promoted promiscuity, abortion, living together before marriage, as well as sexual innuendoes regarding male and female organs and their sizes. Yes, it was that explicit. Violent video games, regardless of the fact they may be animated, are a serious open door for the enemy to gain access to your child's mind. I cannot stress this enough. Many of the violent video games involve the killing of other human beings, physical violence, stealing, coveting. Tread with caution when it comes to video games. By the way, I personally believe Christian adults should be very cautious and proceed with wisdom when it comes to video games.

Use the Ten Commandments as a rule of thumb when it comes to video games. They can be found in Exodus chapter twenty. If the video game, show or movie breaks any of the commandments, it is not safe to participate in. We can also refer to Matthew 12:28-31 "And one of the scribes came up and heard them disputing with one another, and seeing that he answered them well, asked him, 'Which commandment is the most important of all?' [29] Jesus answered, 'The most important is, 'Hear, O Israel: The Lord our God, the Lord is one. [30] And you shall love the Lord your God with all your heart and with all your soul and with all your mind and with all your strength.' [31] The second is this: 'You shall love your neighbor as yourself.' There is no other commandment greater than these.'" If we love our neighbor as ourselves and love God with all our hearts, it will be impossible to envision killing someone or stealing from them. Just imagine, could you partake in these things if Jesus was sitting right next to you? Better yet, could you imagine Jesus playing one of these video games?

As parents our goal and job is to raise disciples of Christ, not children born of the world. Run everything your children do and are exposed to through the filter of Jesus. I've heard people—even Christians—say that protecting our children is putting them in a bubble, and it will make them weak and vulnerable. I disagree. Young minds are impressionable. Remember all those things I was exposed to as a young girl? I was raised in a Roman Catholic family, went to church every Sunday. My parents are still married to each other. We always sat down and had dinner together as a family. We didn't cuss, didn't smoke, and didn't watch filthy television. The things I was exposed to as a child affected my mind, my heart and my spirit. During my junior high and high school years I experienced very challenging times because of the things I had been exposed to. I had sex before marriage. I had a child, unwed, at the age of nineteen, and unfortunately, I had an abortion at the age of twenty-one. No one else in my family went through anything like this. My parents were good parents. I can't say that we studied the Bible as a family. I can't say that Jesus was at the center of our home. Combine this with my childhood experiences, and it was the making of a wounded heart. I will speak more about my abortion experience in a future book.

My point is this, from personal experience, I want to tell you that what we are exposed to as children affects us in many ways and for the rest of our lives. Do everything you can to protect your children. They are not at an intellectually or spiritually developed state to respond to such exposures with wisdom and discipline. Please, do not put this responsibility upon your children. Make the decision for them. Protect them.

Show your children the man, Jesus, and what his character is like. Show them how to model their lives after his. Do this by setting the example. Let your children see you read your Bible. And hear you praying, praising and worshiping. When troubles hit, show them that your first response is reaching out to Abba Father. Not to panic or be anxious for anything (Philippians 4:6-7, Proverbs 31:25). We also want to read the Bible and pray as a family. The family that studies the word and prays together stays together.

Our job as parents, as moms, is to raise strong, Christian, independent adults who can function well in society. By the time they leave our home, they should be fully equipped to make it, knowing they have a safe place in you to go for wisdom and guidance. They should be able to make small mistakes early in the safety of our care, rather than huge mistakes out in the real world.

I remember when our oldest daughter got into a habit of forgetting her lunch. The cafeteria ladies would provide her with a "free" lunch that I eventually had to pay for, or they would give her a free peanut butter and jelly sandwich. She occasionally called me from the office, asking me to bring her lunch. I did that once. Upon discovering this was a habit, I went to the principal and advised that I wanted our daughter to learn a life lesson from this small experience and asked her to partner with us. From that day forward, if our daughter forgot her lunch, she didn't eat until she came home. I believe this may have happened only once before she took the responsibility of making sure she didn't forget her lunch again. This may seem small, but it is a huge lesson that as an adult they need to have conquered.

I will use the same daughter in another example. Back to raising disciples for Christ. When our daughter was in junior high school I dropped her off at school and prayed for her my whole way home. One day, I felt drawn to go to her room and pray for her there. What I saw on her walls and mirror floored me. Tears trickled down my cheeks as my heart melted. Our daughter had tons of scriptures and words of motivation plastered all over her walls and mirror! I was wondering if she had learned anything we had taught her…and there it was. She was listening. She was also walking the walk. I spent time reading the Bible to her as a toddler. We attended church every time the doors were open. I am so thankful I found Jesus before it was too late. She was two years old when we began church. I know for sure that if I hadn't changed my life, her life would've ended up drastically different.

Another example is of our second daughter. She had experienced a major medical setback the past year. She very easily could've fallen into pity party mode, but she didn't. She experiences a great deal of pain from a deep wound on her lower back and has been extremely limited in what she can do, often missing out on activities her siblings participate in. Instead of feeling sorry for herself, she has taken her pain and her experience and turned it into praise and worship of our loving God. She writes music and poetry and sings praise and worship in her room. She draws amazing artwork that glorifies God. This didn't happen by accident. She learned this from watching her parents, her siblings, and church family and from studying the Bible. She spends several hours a day in her room reading, studying, praying, praising and playing the piano or one of her other instruments. Glory to God! This is how we raise disciples.

Our children watch everything we do, say and believe. Whether they ever admit it or not, they look up to us. They want to not only be like us, they want us to like them. They want our approval. Boys especially, want dad's approval. Girls want their mama's approval and daddy's affection. Boys stop falling head over heels for mama around eight years old and start looking up to daddy. They want to mirror his every move. We need to leverage this once-in-a-lifetime opportunity and train them up in the way of the Lord. The only way we can possibly do this is if we are living it! To raise disciples for Christ, we must be disciples ourselves. If we do this, we can rest assured our children will grow up to be strong, god-fearing, adults, ready for whatever comes their way because their rest in the Lord is their weapon.

HOME SCHOOLING

Another favorite topic of mine is home schooling. Our oldest daughter graduated from public school and graduated with honors through the IB (International Baccalaureate) program. She went onto nursing school and graduated summa cum laude as a labor and delivery nurse having landed a job before she even graduated.

I was very involved with her schooling through the public school program. I spent a lot of time up there and paid attention to what was being taught. Our daughter had a successful public school experience all the way through. There were a few things that came up, but they were handled immediately. As our younger children began to enter the public school system, we noticed things that we were not happy with nor did we agree with. We were also becoming more convicted as parents to take the biblical responsibility of training our children up academically. Not all public schools are bad. There are a lot of great teachers out there. I do not want to focus on the negatives of public school, rather the positives of home school.

Because we were seeing a downward trend in the public school setting and because we had some very disappointing experiences with one of our children, we were prompted to consider an alternative education. With my husband deployed to the Middle East, we were limited on family time. When he was home on block leave, we headed back home to Texas and spent time with family. It wasn't long before we were receiving citations in the mail for excessive absences from school. After researching the home school option and attending an event at a local theater where they showed Kirk Cameron's film, *Monumental*, I knew in my heart that we were supposed to home school. We knew this would give us much needed time with daddy, so we began our journey!

Our son was in second grade and our younger daughters were in first and kindergarten when we began. We have been home schooling ever since. We discovered that learning can be very fun and exciting and discovered quickly that learning takes place all day and everywhere. Trips to the grocery store, post office, auto service center, etc. became learning opportunities. Our children spent a great deal of time outside building forts, digging trenches and rivers, building cities out of dirt, and planting gardens. They climbed trees, did yard work, and built things out of wood. Once we moved to our home on twelve wooded, hilly acres our son quickly learned to trap, hunt, skin and tan hides. He learned how to dress his deer, squirrel, rabbit and whatever else he caught. He also learned how to cook the meat! He makes the best squirrel quesadillas! He also took up fishing in the river down the hill. He learned to make great fish tacos. One of our daughters invested a great deal of time in gymnastics. She was very good at it and quickly rose to the top. Home schooling alleviated a lot of stress with regard to time spent on gymnastics.

When daddy was on block leave, we were able to take vacations, go back home, and spend time with family. We didn't have to worry about rushing our children off to school and missing precious time with dad. We would explore somewhere, or just watch a movie together. The time we lost from public school on a daily basis was pretty high once we evaluated it. We realized our children were away from us seven plus hours a day, five days a week. When they came home they often had ten to twelve pages of homework to complete! Half the time they hadn't been taught how to do it, so I would sit down with them and teach them. By the time they were done with their homework, it was time to bathe and go to bed. Something wasn't right. After evaluating the option to home school, my husband and I quickly realized we would not only have more time with our children but we would be the main influence on them instead of liberally indoctrinated agendas that were increasingly showing a disdain for Christianity and America. So, I set out and did my research on all things home school.

I joined every home school Facebook group I could find. I sought out home school moms and asked a LOT of questions. I joined home school groups and sought out cooperative groups. I went on a hunt for the right curriculum and joined Home School Legal Defense Association (HSLDA). I went to home school conventions with my children and we put our eyes and hands on curriculum. I studied my children and their learning types. Then, I studied myself, and how I best learn and how I teach. We began buying curriculum! It was so much fun! The kids were excited and couldn't wait to get started. We set up a classroom. Yes, I made it look like a classroom. This is a little more necessary when you have younger children because you will be doing a lot of group learning and visual teaching with props and manipulatives (tangible tools to assist in learning such as blocks).

We discovered that our home schooling would probably be constantly fluid and ever changing, and that was perfectly alright. The main curriculum we chose we still use today and absolutely love it! It is called My Father's World. This curriculum is biblically based and created for families with multiple children or just one child. We can do group lessons for Bible, history, science, spelling, and some language arts. Then they would do math and writing on their own. As they enter the junior high and high school levels, they are doing more student led individual study. We still conduct group lessons with supplemental curriculum that I added from the Richard Maybury series, "Uncle Eric." Maybury's work focuses on government, history, politics and economics. His book series is amazing and I have personally learned so much.

You may be wondering if home schooling is expensive. It can be. Again, this is another thing I like about My Father's World (MFW). It is affordable, especially for multiple students. The younger children can use a majority of the books and curriculums from the older students, alleviating the costs. All you buy for the younger ones are the consumable products. We do not use the entire suggested curriculum by MFW, however. We have chosen to go with a different curriculum for math, spelling and grammar because that suited our children's learning style. This is very important. It is OK to mix and match curriculum. You want your child's learning experience to be successful and fun. If they are banging their head on the wall whenever it is time to do grammar then that is probably not the right curriculum for them. In fact, each child may require something different, and that is perfectly alright.

It is important to budget for your curriculum ahead of time and have an idea of what and when each child will need it. Your child needs to go at a pace that helps them succeed. One child may excel at math while they struggle with language arts. That is not a problem. One thing you and your children want to get a hold of is that your child needs to go at a pace that is successful for them. If they are not learning or grasping the content, don't move on. Mastery of the content is more important than completing it by a certain time. Goals are great, but mastery is better than deadlines. Some may disagree with this, and that is fine. I would rather my child grasp the concepts than move on and feel lost.

We decided in the very beginning that we would school year-round and take breaks as we need them. In doing this, we never feel guilty if we wake-up one day and everybody is just feeling off and needs a break. We may go for a hike or watch a matinee. Maybe we will go fishing or downtown. Some days we stay home and play games. If you are schooling year-round, this is not a problem at all. We also get to dictate when we take vacations or seasonal breaks. Doing your schooling like this offers many advantages such as cheaper off-season vacations, more family time, attending family celebrations, etc. We also allow our children to work ahead if they are grasping the material. Our youngest daughter is nearly two years ahead in math. She is one-and-a-half grade levels ahead of where she would be if she were in public school. Schooling year-round opens up opportunities for your children to work part-time or do internships. Our son has worked part-time on a ranch since he was thirteen. We calculate his work hours for education hours. He learns a great deal while working, such as building multiple types of fence - including electrical fence and barbed wire fence, working livestock, administering medications to the livestock, and feeding livestock. He learns how to operate large farm equipment such as skid steers and backhoes and he has learned about water pipe repairs, and handling sickly animals. He has learned how to work with people of all ages and backgrounds and how to follow instructions. I think you get the idea. There are so many learning opportunities as homeschoolers. He is discovering what he might want to do for a career, and he is learning what he does not want to do. These hands-on lessons show him the importance of what he is learning in his school lessons.

One of our daughters has had the opportunity to do work studies with a friend of ours who is a zoo keeper. She spent the entire day shadowing her at the zoo, feeding animals, cleaning pens, going to meetings, etc. She quickly discovered that she is good with animals and is very interested in joining their work program for children. To apply for the work program she had to write an essay and answer interview questions on paper. The next step is to do live one-on-one interviews. This will be extremely helpful for her future. Just like our son, she had to work with people of varying ages and follow instructions well.

One of the biggest benefits of home schooling is that children are usually around other children and people of all ages. They are not just around fourth graders. Home schoolers are great at communicating with multi-aged people and adjusting their behavior accordingly. This is such an important skill. They know how to communicate effectively with little children and older adults. This will be incredibly useful as they enter the workforce.

We also have more time in the day to devote to other things such as church, prayer group, play, free-time, hunting, creating, etc. A typical public school day for us was a minimum of seven to eight hours including drop-off and pick-up times. We are free to begin our school day whenever we want. There were times daddy would train over night and be home during the day. So, we did our school training at night and left our days open for daddy. Our typical school day lasts six hours or less. Occasionally our children have taken advantage of this and doubled up on their schoolwork to get ahead. You may be wondering how we have so much free time. Consider the amount of time used in public school to herd large groups of children from one end of the building to the other for bathroom breaks, lunch, PE, recess, etc. This wastes a large amount of time. Then there is the correction of misbehaved students that wastes everyone else's time. Time is wasted moving from class to class. When you home school all of these things are eliminated. We do take lunch breaks and sometimes we'll take breaks to go outside and move around. Our children honestly, just prefer to get their schooling done and be free to do whatever they want the rest of the day.

One of the most important benefits in home schooling is that we have the main influence on our children, and we choose to use a curriculum that is faith based. We also choose a curriculum that teaches our nation's history accurately. This is so important. We place a large emphasis on our Constitution and our Biblical foundation as a nation. A large portion of our curriculum involves Biblical teachings. Our children are getting more Biblical teaching than I had at their age. I encourage you to research curricula and find one that aligns with your family's belief system. I've listed the resources for what we use in the *Recommended Resources* chapter at the back of this book.

Our typical day begins around eight o'clock in the morning. We each spend time in personal Bible study and prayer. We often have breakfast together. Then they begin their lessons while I get my household chores done and do my workout. We do group lessons and eat lunch. I grade their work and go over anything they didn't get right. When they were younger we would do group lessons after breakfast, then they would do their individual subjects, and I assisted as needed.

Know and understand your state's laws for home schooling. Some states are more restrictive than others. Some require a lot of tedious record keeping. Some require a certain number of hours for certain subjects. Some require state standardized testing, while others require no testing. It is also highly recommended that you join the Home School Legal Defense Association (HSLDA). They are your best friend when it comes to home schooling. They know and understand the laws and will represent you if the need ever arises. This happens more than we would hope. They are an excellent resource for all things home school, such as record keeping programs, diplomas, curriculum research, co-op connections, etc. You do not want to go without HSDLA.

You may be interested in finding local co-ops in your area that your children can connect with. There are several different types of co-ops. Some are purely academic. This is for the family who is not doing all of their schooling at home and on their own. Some are a mixture of academic and socialization. Some are purely for socialization or field trip purposes. One thing I quickly learned is that our curriculum was already full enough as it was, and we did not need to add anymore curriculum. So we look for co-ops that were just socialization and/or field trip groups. You also want to take your time investing in a co-op and make sure that they align with your standards and spiritual beliefs. Just because they home school doesn't mean they are devoted Christians. We learned this very fast.

You may be thinking, "I am not qualified to teach my children." Perhaps you are thinking, "There is no way I have the patience to deal with my kids all day, every day." Stop. Let me encourage you right now, you do not need to be an academic scholar to teach your children how to learn. One of my favorite things about home schooling is that we focus on teaching our children how to learn, not just what to learn. Critical thinking is a lost art these days. One of the trademarks of a home school mom is when they are asked a question by their children, we often reply with, "Well, what do you think?" Or, "How do you think is the best way to…?" Another famous one, "Have you looked it up in the dictionary?" We are very slow to give them answers. Rather, we want to show them how to find the answers themselves. One of the main goals of education is to show young people how to find answers and how to come up with their own theories and hypotheses. We do them no services by giving them the answers.

Now, as for the patience situation. I was concerned about the same thing but soon found out I was more at peace home schooling than when we were running frantically everywhere tied by school hours and events. Our entire home was much more peaceful. I had more time to take care of my household chores, to cook, etc. As our children got older I did run into a season (a very short season) where my son and I bumped heads and he was resistant to anything I had to say or anything having to do with school. I did my best to keep my cool, occasionally losing that battle. There may have been an occasion or two where I had to walk out and have some alone time. We worked through it though. Almost every home school child can be threatened with public school and they will shape right up. (This is not to say that we are speaking negatively against public school. We have many friends who attend public school and they are greatly benefiting from it.)

Home schooling does take time, some money, and investment. But, you can do it! It is absolutely worth it. You will not regret it. Find a good support system and be encouraged by them. The benefits far outweigh the negatives. Many colleges are beginning to recognize home schoolers as strong academic additions to their universities, finding that they are already keen on self-discipline and being self-starters. Study habits are already instilled in them, and their drive and determination are noticeable. Their desire to learn and find answers is also very attractive. Yes, home schooled students are great college material. I also want you to know that college is not for everyone, and it is alright if your student would rather attend a trade school or start his own business right out of school, or during school! Society tells us that everyone should go to an expensive college and graduate with a degree, any degree. The home schooling community has been leaning away from this myth and grabbing hold of the truth that you don't have to attend college to be successful...depending on what you want to do in life. If you want to be a surgeon then university is in your future, for a while. But we are recognizing that some students will desire to go into welding, or truck driving. Maybe they want to open a restaurant. They may decide to own and operate a ranch. You do not necessarily need college for that. There are so many trade schools available and so much available online and for free, where they can learn how to do these things.

Times have changed. I would much rather my children go into the field they desire, such as ranching and invest in that ranch and enjoy their career choice than attend college for four years, graduate with a random degree and a whole lot of debt, and find they're not happy with their career field. I cannot tell you how many people I know who fall into this category. I have also seen students from Christian families attend university and fall away from the faith. If we are to think Biblically and eternally minded, then our children's faith and spiritual walk is more important than any degree. Begin helping your children find their passion early on. Watch them. Study them. What are they most interested in and naturally good at? When they start gravitating toward something, help them pursue it. Chances are very high they can begin pursuing their passions before they graduate from high school.

If you have any desire to home school your children and the only thing holding you back is lack of confidence, move forward! Join those co-ops and home school groups. Get to know other home schoolers and rely on their wisdom and experience. You can home school!

HOMEMAKING
EVERY HOUSE CAN BE A HOME

No matter where you live or what kind of structure you live in, it can be made into a home. I remember when my husband entered the Army after 9/11, and we were stationed on the east coast in base housing. Our oldest daughter was in fourth grade, our son was just about six months old, and I was pregnant with our next daughter. We had no idea what to expect.

The military moved our belongings while we brought our necessities with us. We had no idea it would take over four weeks to receive our household goods. When we arrived on base, they gave us the keys to our new "home." Only, it wasn't very new at all. In fact, it was probably built somewhere in the mid sixties with a lot of traffic in and out before us. It was a three bedroom cinder block house with the ugliest dark brown paint. It was so dreary. The wood doors and trim had been recently lacquered for probably the hundredth time, maybe even the day before. The aroma was heavy and made us dizzy. The house had that infamous 1960's linoleum tile flooring, the whole house, even the bedrooms. And there was ONE bathroom. A pregnant mama with a husband and two children and…ONE…bathroom.

This house did not seem like a home. Well, maybe for the "palmetto bugs" that lived there. These people tried to convince us that they were not cockroaches but, "palmetto bugs." Friend, they were cockroaches. In fact, they were cockroaches so big that your kids could ride them to school. They had their own shadows! They were HUGE! So, for four weeks we went to war with the "palmetto bugs" while eagerly awaiting our household goods. We made the best of the times.

Finally, we received our household goods (military term for belongings) and began decorating. We were on an E5 salary so money was tight. Still, we found a way to decorate and make that horrid structure our home. I made sure we had beautiful comforters on our beds and our things were neatly organized and not strewn all over the place. You can find really inexpensive furniture to refurbish at Goodwill or second hand shops. I found some very affordable sheer curtains at Walmart and rugs to cover that awful tile. We would light candles (thankfully there was no explosion from the lacquer fumes). I always used the best smelling detergent I could find, especially for our linens, and diligently vacuumed and mopped the house weekly and more often if necessary. That house became our home. We took care of what we had. While the structure itself looked like a prison, the inside looked and felt like a home. Then I planted rose bushes outside and other blooming plants to liven up the exterior.

    The most important thing you can do to make your house feel like a home is to keep it clean and organized. Nothing screams discomfort and disorder louder than a filthy and cluttered home. When you walk into a home like that, you physically feel uncomfortable. It causes the mind and emotions to feel tense. This is such a simple solution. Take care of your home. Clean it. Organize it. Pick up after yourself and train your children to do the same. Every little piece of clutter adds to the tension. Re-evaluate your belongings. Do you really need it? Do you really use it? My rule of thumb is, if we haven't used it in at least six to twelve months, it is given away, sold, or thrown out.

First, decide the purpose for each room and decorate accordingly. If you have a dining room that will be used for eating, create an atmosphere that is pleasant to dine in. No one wants to eat a meal with a tower of bills stacked in front of them, or dog food bowls sitting next to their plate.

Your living room is not your laundry room. Don't allow dirty or clean clothes to pile up on your couch.

The kitchen is not your garage. Don't get in the habit of storing tools and things on the counter.

Do you get the idea? Decide the purpose for each room and decorate around that theme. Your bathroom should be like a spa or sanctuary. It should be a place where you can go and get alone, get clean, rejuvenate and refresh your mind, body, and spirit. If your bathroom is junked up with half used or empty bottles of everything under the sun, it loses that inviting atmosphere. It screams, "Hurry up and get out!" If you don't have cabinets to put things in, find some shelving or canisters to organize your things for the bathroom. Whatever you do, keep that counter clear with minimal stuff. Twenty bottles of lotion sitting out is not necessary. Choose one and put the others away. Personal hygiene items are best stored in a cabinet or canister, especially for a guest bathroom.

Have blankets available throughout the home, especially if you tend to maintain a cooler temperature. This will help guests feel more comfortable while visiting. Another way to make your home inviting is to decorate! Decorate for the seasons and holidays. Even if you have to hand-make (which is a lot of fun!) your decorations, consider doing it. The children love it and it creates tradition. Have your children participate. Show them how to make a house a home. Again, stay away from cluttering your house up with too much. Often minimal is better. You don't want to walk into a room that feels like autumn just vomited a ton of leaves. It should be peaceful, not overwhelming.

Another thing I want to touch on is television. I highly encourage you to not have your televisions constantly running. I hear people talk about background noise. If you constantly need background "noise," there may be a personal issue to address. This is an indication that you are trying to drown out some thoughts. Constant noise is nerve-wracking to the mind. It is good practice to be content in the silence. If there is constant noise it is difficult to hear the voice of the Lord. If the television is constantly on, it often distracts from what could be engaging conversation and fellowship. I cannot tell you how many times I've been to someone's house and they often have the television on. I see people fixated on the television and disengaged in their company. This is awkward for your company and damaging to your relationship with your family. I encourage you to set aside time for personal quiet time. This could be a time for personal reading, prayer, family bible study, etc. We went over nine years without a television set in our home.

We did not subscribe to cable or satellite. Every now and then we would watch something on a streaming service. While our children were younger though, we did not spend a lot of time watching television and this was a tremendous asset in our children's lives. They learned the importance of fellowship, family time, and being creative with your time. This also prevented them from exposure to ungodly shows and commercials. Their minds were not desensitized to ungodly content. When we visit someone with television and see the commercials, we are stunned at what has become acceptable. Instead of television we spend time outdoors enjoying God's creation. We cook together and play lots of card and board games.

Another way to make any place a home is how we treat one another. We must show each other love, grace, mercy, respect and gentleness. When I was a young mom I tended to yell a lot. I was often stressed out and high strung. Mothers, wives, our attitude and behavior often sets the tone for the home. Our goal is to create a peaceful and safe atmosphere, not one our children are always looking to escape. When our children slip-up, let's love them through it and show them grace and mercy. We need to teach them how to recover from mishaps. Our homes should be the safest place for them to make mistakes and learn from them. When we are disappointed in someone's behavior, raising our voices is not the appropriate response. Lashing out in anger is not suitable. If you feel that you are about to respond with high emotions, take a few moments and get alone, pray, sing praises to the Lord.

Ask the Lord to show you how to respond. Whatever you do, find a way to make your home a place where you speak softly, love tenderly, and pray fervently.

Lastly, have Bibles available throughout your home. While this is not last because it lacks importance, it is last because I want to leave on this note. Have multiple types of Bibles available to meet the needs of young children, learning readers, and adults. Set a family bible study time each day. We would read as a family at night before bed and say prayers together. When dad was deployed or away, he would often try to join us via phone call. We traditionally let the youngest go first and dad concludes. We take turns reading a chapter each night. The best way to make a house a home is to invite the Lord in and let him be the head of the home in every area. Make sure your home is a safe place where mistakes can be made without fear of punishment but with grace, mercy, love and when necessary, discipline. Discipline and punishment are two different things. Punishment is done from a posture of anger and fear. Discipline is done from a posture of love. When the Lord is the head of a home, your home will be a comforting, safe place not only for your family, but also for many others.

I asked my cousin, Lauren Grumbles, to share some of her expertise with us. Lauren is a designer, and a very talented one at that. You can find more about her work at **www.laurengrumbles.com**.

Professional Design Tips:-

-Hang drapery panels as high as the wall allows in rooms that have a ceiling height less than ten feet. Oftentimes the top of the window is still a few feet below the ceiling and when curtains are hung just at the top of the window, the opportunity to heighten a room is lost. By hanging your rod and curtains around four to six feet below the ceiling/crown molding, the vertical line of the drapery creates a visual cue that the room is taller than it is. This trick can create the feel of space in tight quarters as well as giving you more surface area to incorporate color, pattern and texture.

-Make sure the drapery panels extend all the way down to the floor, within one inch of touching the floor. When drapery hangs higher than that, the effect is that the drapery is too short for the wall. If you have a hard time finding extra long drapery to accomplish this effect, consider adding a decorative contrast fabric to the bottom of store-bought curtains. It's a great way to add a pop of color or pattern to a solid drapery fabric using the most basic sewing skills. Another way to create a custom drapery look is to buy solid panels and add your own pattern with fabric paint and large scale stencils (helpful tip: if you opt to paint your own fabric, pre-wash the curtains first and use a very light application of paint so that the drapery will wash and hang well over time).

-When purchasing a rug, buy the largest rug that space and budget afford. Contrary to popular belief, larger rugs will make the room feel more spacious and anchor the furniture that is sitting on it even if covers a portion of a lovely wood floor. If a large area rug isn't in your budget, check out a retail carpet supplier and ask to see their remnant pieces. Those pieces can be cut and bound to the perfect size, often at a fraction of the cost. If you are renting or have unsightly flooring, a large area rug gives you an added bonus of a clean and comfortable place to spend time with your family if you are short on seating.

-Lighting can be the unexpected hero or villain in any room and most homes do not come wired for adequate and pleasing light. In any given space, you need to have multiple sources of light. This means that the bulb hanging from your ceiling fan isn't going to cut it. Add in table lamps and floor lamps in two to three spaces around the room to keep an even distribution of light as well as a warm and inviting space to gather with your family. The quality of the light is important too and not all bulbs are created equal. Incandescent bulbs are most common and while they're not the most energy efficient, they are by far the most complimentary to our skin tone and psychologically appealing (we look good and feel good). If you're looking to be more energy efficient, make sure you find an LED or Compact Fluorescent bulb that has "color correction" so you don't end up with a cold, hospital room vibe.

-Painting walls can be an expensive and overwhelming exercise. Here are some tips to make the best of your effort:

Color: Oftentimes a homeowner will have a color in mind for what they want, take a trip to the paint store and pick out that color from the most vibrant section of the paint swatches. This can result in a color that is too intense for most residential environments and better served for commercial and hospitality spaces (think restaurants and shopping centers). My advice is to find the "neutral" area of the paint samples and then look for your color there. Even within those more subtle areas, you'll find all the shades of the rainbow in a more livable version.

Sampling: If you've ever been bitten by the paint bug you know how tempting it is to get the paint on the wall as soon as possible! The biggest mistake I see homeowners make however, is rushing the selection process and either skipping the sample stage all together or not sampling the paint adequately. Once you've visited the paint store, go home with several small swatches to narrow down the right color for your space. Once you've narrowed it down to two or three options, buy the smallest can available and paint the samples on large white poster boards (one color per board). The large size allows you to get a true representation of what the color looks like and the movable nature of the poster board allows you to pin it up on different walls with different exposures throughout the day and night. Once you've done the sample work, live with the samples for a few days. Viewing a sample in both natural day-light and incandescent lamp light will ensure that you don't end up with a color that shines during the day and looks like pea-soup at night. Yes, this seems like an exhaustive effort…but trust me, once you've either labored through an entire paint job yourself or paid for professional services, the last thing you want to feel is regret.

Prep, prep, prep: A small investment in time and money will ensure that all of your hard work looks like a million bucks. Remove electrical plates completely from the wall, dust and then tape off baseboards and trim work, lay down tarps and paint barefoot so you can feel if you step in a drip before you track it all over your house.

CLEANLINESS AND ORGANIZATION

One of my favorite topics and activities is cleaning and organizing. Yes, you read that right! Sounds strange, doesn't it? But the end result is so rewarding. It's like vacuuming yourself out of a room and then seeing how beautiful the floor looks. The same concept exists with mowing your lawn. It just looks crisp, clean, and welcoming.

Picture an overgrown garden full of dying plants, weeds, stickers and briars. You aren't too excited about walking into that are you? But when you come across a garden that is vibrant, well kept, and full of color and beauty, you want to spend time there! The same goes for a home. When your home is clean and organized, people want to hang out there. That is what we are going for!

There is cleaning, and there is deep cleaning. Anytime we move into a new house (which has been often as a military family) the very first thing I do is go in before moving day and deep clean the entire house from top to bottom.

- Dust fan blades, the top frames of doors, thermostat boxes, air filter grids, curtain rods, window sills, cabinets, tops of refrigerators, etc.
- Pull out every single appliance and get down on my hands and knees and get rid of all the junk, dirt, and filth.
- Vacuum away the dust and dirt first, then, get Clorox bleach and scrub away every piece of evidence of previous ownership.
- Scrub down the back and sides of the appliances and the floor and side of the cabinets where the appliance fits.
- Use the same process to scrub out every single cabinet and closet in the entire house. Diligently scrub the bathrooms from top to bottom with bleach.
- Scrub the counters, sinks, showers and bathtubs multiple times and rinse out with the hottest possible water.
- Scrub the toilets from top to bottom, from the outside to the inside.

Since I will never use these cleaning supplies again, I toss them out. In fact, if the house is really gross, I will use a cheap old vacuum cleaner the first time around, then throw it out. Have the carpets professionally shampooed. Scrub all of the hard surface flooring multiple times with disinfectant and then polish them. Again, toss these mops out and don't use them again. Scrub all the baseboards with Clorox (Or, whatever cleaner you choose) and vacuum again. Remove the blinds and screens and wash them out thoroughly with hot soapy water and disinfectant. I typically don't keep window treatments from previous owners unless I can tell they were very clean. Even then, I wash them. Scrub out the window sills thoroughly. Polish all of the wood in the house as well. This rejuvenates the wood and restores it to nearly original status. Wood that is losing its shine is drab, and polishing is such an easy fix. I deep clean our home like this at least once a quarter.

The refrigerator gets deep cleaned once a month, period. Everything gets pulled out, including the drawers and trays and I scrub it down. Discard anything that is out of date. I keep our refrigerator very organized. Again, inviting is best. You don't want your refrigerator to be a hot mess. Things need to be easily found. One of my favorite elementary teachers had a catchy saying, "Everything has a place and in its place everything should be." I have lived by this rule ever since. It is a terrific rule. Teach it to your children. It applies to everything, not just the fridge. It is also a health concern when old food particles are allowed to grow bacteria in our fridge. The bacteria can spread, contaminating other food. For this reason it is important to throw out foods that are out of date or visibly growing mold. One of the few exceptions is cheese. You can simply cut past the mold and still use the good parts.

The stove, oven, and dryer are very important appliances that require a monthly deep cleaning. House fires are often caused by dirty stovetops and ovens or dyers filled with lint. When you allow grease and grime to build-up under the burners (traditional electric or gas) or inside the oven, that grease and grime can actually catch fire when it gets to cooking too hot. The same is true for dryers that have been collecting lint for long periods of time. That lint heats up during use and can

> **LAUNDRY RULES**
>
> - Button, zip, snap & fasten all hardware on clothing
> - Remove all chapstick & toothpicks
> - Remove all change
> - **Remove** all live ammunition
> - **Remove** all live explosives
>
> Thank you,
>
> Management

easily catch fire. Deep cleaning your stove, oven and dryer are first and foremost a safety precaution. Secondly, it is for the sake of good health. Food particles that are sitting even a short period of time can grow harmful bacteria. Besides it is not very appetizing to see old food caked onto the cooking surfaces. When I am invited to dinner at someone's house, honestly, if their home is dirty, especially their kitchen and bathroom, I lose my appetite. These are easy things to fix and manage.

For the lighter, daily cleaning I do something similar. By the way, I begin teaching our children at a very early age that they not only can help clean, but they are expected to. They are responsible for their bedroom and bathroom area from the time they are mobile. Before they can get another toy out, they must first put away the previous one. They are trained that, "Everything has a place and in its place everything should be." This also avoids constantly misplacing things and makes it easier for others to find things because they are always where they should be. This is especially important for first aid, medical supplies, keys, fire extinguishers, etc.

    Back to daily cleaning. One of the best things you can do is get a hold of that phrase above and make it a household rule. If you can do this, it will make your life so much easier. It also makes the house so much more organized. If you eliminate the daily clutter, that eliminates a large portion of cleaning. I very rarely go to bed with dishes in the sink. If I do, it is because they are drying. But typically, I will put them away. It literally takes seconds. I do not want to wake-up in the morning and already have chores to do that could have been done the night before. The same concept goes for leaving the house. The last thing I want to do is return home and have to start cleaning right away. I make every effort to leave a tidy home.

I clean as I cook. I have taught the children to do the same. This also makes it easier at the end when you're tired from all that cooking. This makes for a safer cooking environment also.

We clean up after ourselves in the bathroom and do not leave dirty clothes or towels on the floor, or hair in the tub. We flush our toilets. (You might be surprised; some people will only flush their toilet every so often.) Please, flush your toilet. This will also eliminate that awful urine ring around the bowl as well as the stench that comes with it. Gross.

If we cuddle up with a blanket, we fold it and put it away when we are done. We do not leave drinking glasses out over night. We do not leave dirty dishes in the sink. It is too easy and quick to either clean it and put it in the drying rack or rinse it and put it in the dishwasher. There is no reason to leave food stained dishes out. If you can do these things it will make your cleaning so much easier. A note about the husband who might leave dirty dishes "soaking" in the sink, wives just take care of those dishes for him. Remember, he has worked hard all day to provide for you and your children. The least you can do is joyfully serve him by cleaning his dishes without complaining. I used to get so frustrated about this, but the Lord showed me a better way. It is my honor to wash his dishes after he's had a hard, long day at work.

I dust, Clorox the kitchen and bathrooms, vacuum and mop once a week, more as needed. Clean from top to bottom. (Have you seen the movie, *Annie*?) Your floors should be done last. A clean home is a healthy and peaceful home. It usually only takes me about two to three hours. Dusting includes everything you can see - picture frames, tops of appliances, bookshelves, mantles, collectibles, etc. When I deep clean, I vacuum under and behind furniture. I get under the recliners and beds. When my children were younger I purposely left certain chores for discipline. For instance, if they were being disrespectful I would let them wash and scrub the baseboards or dust every leaf of a plant, or every blind on every window. These are tasks that are tedious for me but need to be done.

At this point you may think a lot of this is overkill. Maybe, but it sure has made for a comfortable, inviting home that we appreciate and enjoy living in. It has also kept us healthy. So many families are always sick. I go to their house and see why. Their house is filthy! There are thick layers of dust everywhere, really old dirty dishes in the sink or on the couch. Their bathrooms...oh...their bathrooms. Let's just say, I did not use them. A clean, organized home is a happy, healthy home.

We have a rule in our house (a certain child is still learning) that we make our beds as soon as we wake-up. We do not allow our beds to remain unmade throughout the day. This not only looks sloppy but is also lazy. We must care for and manage well what we have been blessed with. Not to mention, at night who wants to get into a sloppy, cold bed. When you make your bed neatly each day it is so much more inviting to get into a clean bed at night. Your linens should be washed at least once every two weeks, preferably every week. As we sleep we sweat and our bodies shed particles. That is really gross isn't it? Well, all the sweat and particles gather in your sheets. They create odors. I know you have recognized the fresh, inviting scent of freshly washed linens. Why do you think they don't stay smelling that fresh? Wash your linens often. Our family is in the habit of bathing before we get into our beds, even if we bathed that morning. During the day your body collects particles from the environment, including sweat. We want to be clean when we get into our beds. Your comforter or bedspread should be washed at least once a month. Yes, I actually wash our comforter once a month. It is so delightful climbing into those freshly washed linens! In fact, the fresh linen aroma permeates our entire bedroom! On a side note, did you know that most hotels do not wash the comforters after every guest? I used to work at a large hotel in Dallas, TX. When I found that out, I never keep the comforter on the bed.

Shoes. Ever since we had little babies we stopped wearing shoes in the house. I did some research before making this call. What I discovered was amazingly disgusting! Most European and Asian countries, and Hawaiian's remove their shoes before entering their homes. It is not just about respect. It actually has a lot to do with health and cleanliness. This particular subject could really fit in several chapters of this book. Think about all the places you have walked with your shoes on. Public restrooms, gas stations, doctors' offices, hospitals, Walmart, public school buildings, work places, your backyard where your dogs freely poop and pee, your ranch or farm, etc. Need I say more? That is pretty gross when you think about it. Do you want your babies crawling on and licking that floor? Do you want to walk barefoot on that floor and then get into your freshly cleaned bed? I hope not!

Not only is it unsanitary to wear shoes inside the home it also causes more housework. The more people wear shoes inside your house, the more often you will need to sweep or vacuum and mop. Our family likes to sit on the floor a lot, especially during lessons or prayer. Would you want to sit on the floor of a public restroom? I know I sure wouldn't. And yes, we ask our guests to remove their shoes before entering our home. We have plenty of closets and shoe racks available to store them. We also offer socks to those who don't want to go barefoot. Most of our close friends know this about us and come prepared. In fact, many of them have started doing this in their own homes. When it comes to maintenance people, you definitely want them removing their shoes if at all possible. Sometimes electricians must keep theirs on for safety reasons. In these circumstances I provide them with hospital style booties to put over their shoes and then throw them out. Don't let them use their own because they have most likely used them at other people's homes. Trust me, get your own disposable booties. They can be found at

Lowes, Walmart, or online from a medical supply store. It may seem tedious or difficult to retrain your brain to remove shoes, but in my opinion, it is well worth it. Again, our family is hardly ever sick. Also, this preserves the life of your hard surface floors and carpeted areas.

While on the subject of removing shoes before entering the home let's discuss animals. We personally prefer animals not to be inside unless they are aquarium/cage animals. However, I know many people disagree with this and that is perfectly all right. We used to allow dogs in our home, but wouldn't allow them in the kitchen or dining areas. After I started cooking for a business we quit letting the dogs in. If you choose to have your pets inside, I would suggest at least not allowing your animals in the kitchen and dining area. We don't want our guests to discover dog hair in their food. More than that, it is a sanitary issue. For the same reason we remove our shoes to keep all that nastiness from outside and public places from entering our home, it is important to consider your pets' feet. Animals do not have the sense to avoid walking in urine, dog poop, vomit, etc. In fact, most animals lick the stuff! Do you really want that all over your floors and furniture? Animals carry bacteria and diseases. We do not want to include these things in our food. When dogs or cats walk around they shed dander and pet hair which flies around, landing on counter tops and tables. It didn't take us but a few days to get our dogs trained to not enter the kitchen or dining area when we used to allow them indoors. My husband agreed that it was cleaner to just keep them outside unless there was an extreme weather condition. In those cases they were allowed into the laundry room or maybe the living room, but not the kitchen and dining area.

Don't forget about changing those air vents on a regular monthly schedule and while you're up there vacuum out the grates and air intakes and outflows. Also, keep up the routine maintenance on your AC/Heating unit. This is extremely important for preserving the life of your air and heating unit as well as your air ducts. It is also crucial for your family's health. Constant dust and air pathogen build-up can cause an array of illnesses and allergies that can easily be avoided by changing out your filters and keeping your vents clean. On this topic, whenever you get an opportunity to open those windows and let fresh air come in, do it! This is so good for your home and your family. Natural sunlight also kills germs and gives the body energy and nutrients. I want to encourage you to open your blinds and curtains whenever possible. Letting in natural light is not only good for the home and your body, but it's good for your mind too. Natural sunlight is up-lifting. Also, when we see that there is beauty and life going on outside we tend to be more motivated to get out there and get our body moving. A house which has the blinds closed all the time is dark and dreary and a major mood killer and energy sucker.

    Speaking of getting outside, I want to remind you that your vehicles are an extension of your home. Our vehicles are under our care and responsibility as well. Just like the home, it is important to keep them clean, organized and running smoothly. Routine maintenance is just as important for your vehicle as it is for your home appliances. Just like collected dust particles and air pathogens are in the home, they are harmful in your vehicle as well. It is very important to keep your vehicle organized and clutter free. Loose objects will become projectile missiles during an accident. They can also obstruct the driver's view and ability to recover from an accident. When I was in high school I was riding with a friend who drove a Volkswagen Bug. My box purse had been loosely sitting on the seat and found its way to the driver's side floorboard...under the brake pedal. It was a rainy day and we approached a red light. The Ford sign on the back of the truck in front of us kept getting bigger and bigger as we all yelled at my friend, "STOP!" She barked back, "I CAN'T!" She couldn't stop the vehicle because a loose item (mine) had lodged its way under the brake, impeding her from to safely stopping the vehicle. Secure loose items in your vehicles.

While we're outdoors, let's discuss lawn maintenance. Some husbands prefer to do the yard work themselves, mine does. In fact, this has almost become a battle between us, because we both enjoy doing it so much. When we lived on our small ranch in Texas, I enjoyed riding the John Deere. It was my sanctuary time. Just like vacuuming, I enjoy seeing the finished product of a nicely manicured lawn. So does my husband. Nonetheless, the lawn must be maintained. If you have older children who are responsible enough to handle a push mower or riding mower and weed eater, this is a great time to teach them responsibility and team work. They need to learn to put work and effort into the place they live as well. They should be taught from a very early age that each person plays a part in the upkeep of the home. Everyone should carry their weight and not expect a free ride. This instills responsibility and maturity as well as know-how for when they are young adults and on their own. Some pointers on lawn care - When you mow, mow so that the blower is facing away from the windows and the house. Otherwise, loose rocks and other hard objects can become little missiles that break windows, and that costs money (possibly said from experience.) Same thing around flower beds and gardens so grass is not being blown into those areas. Not only does this cause more clean-up, but those grass blades can carry grass seeds which can transfer to your garden, where you do not want grass growing. Look up your area's zone for planting and plant things that will bloom at various times of year creating a pleasant and beautiful yard. This is not only pleasant for your neighbors, but it will draw you and your family outdoors more. That is a good thing!

Finally, regarding maintenance, I want to suggest that you get yourself a really good tool kit and a level.

Keep the following items on hand:

hair picks	duct tape
hair bands	electrical tape
rubber bands	Gorilla glue

wood glue
rubber cement
Goo Gone
clear and white caulking
caulking gun
wall repair paste
rubber bands-all sizes and widths
batteries of every size
flashlights
light bulbs
Q-Tips
plunger
a couple of boxes of rubber gloves
tweezers
scissors (that will not be used on the human body)
rubbing alcohol
white distilled vinegar
apple cider vinegar
old rags and towels
set of work clothes
drop cloths
touch up paint
Drano
WD-40

I have probably missed a lot. These are all things that will come in very handy for all sorts of home repair jobs. Trust me.

FAMILY HEALTH

Family health is so important. As a wife and mother, you have more control of your family's health than you may realize. I am not looking for a debate on any of these topics and respect your right to view things differently. I am sharing my view and opinions of what has worked for our family, which are not on a "professional" level. I am not a licensed or certified nutritionist, doctor, nurse, or pharmacist, but I am a nationally certified personal trainer with a focus on Biomechanics of Resistance Training, Special Populations, and Food and Nutrition Guidance. I have received certifications from: Cooper Institute for Aerobics Research, Brett Auberg, NASM, and ACE.

      I have done a lot of research, experienced a lot of medical situations, and have learned from trial and error. Anything that I say in this book is not meant to be taken as medical advice, and I waive all responsibility of harm or injury by you or anyone you know following any of what I share in this book. It is highly recommended that you do your own research and seek medical advice before using any remedies shared here. I am only sharing what our family does and what has and hasn't worked.

We have chosen not to vaccinate our children after we were forced to in the military. After our youngest was five years old, we no longer sought vaccinations for our children. We choose to not get the flu vaccine. We refused the Gardasil vaccine for our oldest daughter when it first came out, and we are so glad we did, seeing that it may cause cancer in some individuals. Our doctors are very supportive of this decision and our family over all is very healthy. We very seldom go to the doctor for minor illnesses or injuries. We choose to use homeopathic and other remedies at home first, and if something serious occurs, we do not hesitate to see our doctor or visit the emergency room. We are not opposed to medicine or health care, but practice preventive care first.

I spoke on some of this in the previous chapter regarding cleanliness and organization. The cleaner you keep your home, the less illness you will experience. I recall being stationed on the east coast and we had a neighbor in base housing whose children were always ill. In fact, her toddlers often showed up across the street at our house pounding on the door to be let in and fed. This particular military spouse's husband was deployed at the time. Unfortunately, she was addicted to meth. One day her precious little boy showed up at our door. He was filthy and starving. I took him and went over to his house, knocking on the door, for his mom. No answer. I went inside calling for her. Nothing.

As I went through the house what I discovered was nothing short of awful. The house was absolutely filthy. There was old food sitting out everywhere with maggots making their home in it. There were items that required refrigeration that had obviously been sitting out for who knows how long. Human feces were smeared on the walls and dirty diapers breeding maggots, randomly lay around the house. The bathrooms were horrendous! The bathtubs looked like they had never been cleaned and were filled with black filth. This was brand new housing by the way, not even a year old. There were roaches crawling in broad daylight. Needless to say, the authorities were called, and all of her children were removed from the home. The children were sick and malnourished. Filthiness leads to sickness. Please, keep your home clean. For further help on how to maintain a healthy home and environment see the chapter titled, "Cleanliness and Organization."

I have also included information on healthy eating and cooking in the previous chapter as well as in the, "Favorite Recipes," chapter. To reiterate, it is best to use all-natural and organic foods whenever possible. So many chemicals, additives, hormones, antibiotics and other junk is put into food. Do what you can to stay away from processed foods. I realize there are occasions that this may be the only way to feed your family. Sparingly used, it will not be too harmful. Learn what foods are good for health and curing illnesses and diseases. See the "Recommended Resources" chapter for some great books on this subject.

I keep certain home remedies stocked and readily available. They are safe for our children and they know how to use them responsibility in case of an emergency.

We abide by the rule, "Everything has a place and in its place everything should be." This is crucial for this topic. You never want to be in a crisis situation in need of medical supplies, and they are not where they should be. Keep up with the shelf life of your medicinal products. Know if the expiration date is a hard date or more of a "cover-the-manufacturer" date. EpiPens have more of a "cover-the-manufacturer" date. Our pharmacist told us that as long as the liquid in the window is clear it is safe to use. If it is anything other than clear, don't use it and discard it. Considering the outrageous price of EpiPens, I am personally holding on to as many of them as I can for as long as their liquid is clear.

Read the labels of beverages (and all food). If there are a lot of words ending in, "ose," proceed with caution. Soda. Caffeinated drinks. Unhealthy. There is no way around it, soda is so bad for your health. It is full of sugars and other ingredients that are terrible for your body, digestive system and teeth, especially baby teeth. Have you considered that you can use a soda to clean off the acid from a corroded car battery to enable you to start the engine? Do you really want that going into your child's body? Many juices are the same as soda.

Elderberry syrup or gummies along with Doterra's On Guard capsules and oil for the diffuser are among the things on the recommended supply list. Anytime we are around people who are sick, or we feel like we may be coming down with something we take this combination: Two On Guard capsules the first time and one every four hours after that. We will take 2 tbsp of elderberry syrup or four gummies at first, and then 1 tbsp or two gummies every four hours. If we really feel like something more than a cold coming on like strep throat or tonsillitis, or some other powerful illness not requiring medical attention, we will use the homeopathic concoction for an antibiotic. This can be found in the book, *Be Your own Doctor*, in the recommended reading list at the back of this book. This is a very powerful, natural antibiotic that will knock stuff out fast. Be warned though, it is not pleasant tasting, so mix it with some juice. Another alternative is to use the tincture, Heal All.

For venomous bites, cellulitis or skin infections we use charcoal paste. You can now easily find charcoal powder or even paste in the hygiene section of any major store or Walmart. If you are unable to find it in a store, you can find it on-line. If you get the powder form, simply mix it with a small amount of water to create a thick paste. Take a black pen or permanent marker and draw a circle around the red, infected area and write the date and time outside of the circle. Then put a liberal amount of paste directly on the infected area and extend it out about a centimeter or more.

    Cover the area completely with a gauze bandage and tape the edges securely for twenty-four hours, at the end of twenty-four hours remove the bandage and inspect it for infected puss or drainage, then inspect the infected area. If it still shows signs of redness or swelling, repeat the procedure and re-inspect the area in twenty-four hours. So far, we have only had to go forty-eight hours until an infection has been completely healed. Taking care of skin infections is crucial, because they can easily and quickly become infected and cause sepsis to form within the body and/or blood stream. This is very dangerous. If you cannot get an infection under control within forty-eight hours or if you see red streaking in the infected area or it is warm to the touch, or the patient is showing any other signs of severe infection such as vomiting, persistent headache, changes in blood-pressure, fever, etc, seek medical attention immediately.

Home remedies and First-Aid:

- Elderberry syrup and gummies
- OnGuard by Doterra essential oil capsules
- OnGuard Doterra essential oil
- OnGuard lozenges by Doterra
- Doterra Ginger lozenges (For stomach upset)
- Dramamine
- Dramamine Naturals (safe for children)
- Charcoal paste
- Blood stop
- Wound spray
- Sovereign Silver Hydrosol
- Heal All tincture
- Extract of Cayenne
- Extract of Hyssop
- Extract of Turmeric
- Extract of Jewelweed
- Tylenol
- Advil
- Baby Aspirin
- Rubbing alcohol
- Peroxide
- White distilled vinegar
- Apple cider vinegar
- Salt
- Extensive First-aid kit
- Flashlights with back-up batteries
- Tourniquets
- Buckets for vomiting
- Rubber gloves
- Syringe med droppers
- EpiPens
- Yellow Mustard (Vomit inducer)
- Baking soda

Super glue (For closing deep wounds not requiring stitches)
Simple splints
Crutches
Ace bandages
Sleeping cot (For keeping an eye on sick children)

Fire extinguishers (ABC) on every floor the kitchen, and at least one outside.
Window ladder for 2nd floor fire escape

I hope that I included everything in the above list. However, I encourage you to research what you need for your household in case of an emergency. I also strongly advise you and your spouse to get CPR-First Aid certified, and learn the proper use of fire extinguishers. Once your children are mature, have them get certified as well. Create a safety and emergency preparedness plan for your family and household. This should include a map of your home and neighborhood, including all possible exits, neighbors' homes, to include safe neighbors that your children can go to for help.

It is a good idea to know which neighbors you can trust and have a plan in place before a crisis hits. A crisis plan should be discussed with your neighbors and practiced. You want your children familiar with how to respond. Practicing emergency preparedness alleviates mistakes and fear. It is also a great idea to role-play and practice various scenarios with your children. I did this with our children and we not only had a lot of fun but their preparedness has been put to the test multiple times and they passed with flying colors!

Back in 2014 our son experienced a major ranching accident. We would haul round bales in our one ton dually pick-up to the pasture. To get through the gate, the girls would run the sheep and pigs off and our son opened the gate as I drove through. Then they'd all jump on the back and we would drive out. This time however, was different. I thought our son had jumped on the side, so I began driving. I started hearing what sounded like giggling and wondered what he was up to this time, as he was always joking around. It got louder. I looked in my side mirror and there was my son, almost completely under my left two rear tires! His body lay in the fetal position. He was not giggling. He was crying and screaming, "Get off me! Get off me!"

  I had stopped, why did I stop? I didn't know if I should drive forward or backward, what would injure him the most? I quickly just drove forward and slammed it into park and jumped out. He wasn't moving. His watery eyes just stared at me and he begged me, "Mom, help me…" Our daughters were panicking and screaming. I told one of them to run for the neighbor and the other to go grab blankets for her brother, then stand by the street waiting for the ambulance. This gave them purpose and direction, which alleviated panic. I had already dialed 911. I looked him in the face and began a series of questions:

"Does it hurt to breathe?"

He barely shook his head, "No."

"Can you move?"

He whispered, "No."

I asked, "Can you move your legs and feet?"

He shook his head, "No."

Trying to disguise my concern, "Can you feel your legs and feet?"

My son slowly shook, "No."

The dispatcher answered. Quickly but with clarity, I gave our address. I proceeded, "Ten year old boy, ran over by one ton dually and a thousand pound round bale. Conscious and breathing. Can't move his body. No feeling from waist down. Beginning to go into shock. We're not moving him. Internal organ status unknown. Please hurry."

The dispatcher said responders were on their way and asked if there was a clear landing for a helicopter. I told her they could land in our pasture. The dispatcher remained on the line. Our neighbor arrived with our daughter. She called my husband for me. I sent our daughter inside to gather clothes for her and her sister to stay with our neighbor. Fire trucks, paramedics, and police cars arrived swiftly. Our neighborhood looked like a crime scene. As I briefed them, they checked him thoroughly. I stood behind him with my hands on his head praying out loud, begging God to save his life and preserve his organs. The firefighters cut his muck boots off and were checking him thoroughly.

The lead paramedic approached me, "Ma'am, he seems to be fine?" He was confused. He proceeded to tell me that every organ and bone appeared to be intact but suggested he go to the emergency room just to be sure. There they could do X-rays and MRI's.

I asked him if he was sure he was O.K. He confirmed. I shouted so loud, "Thank you Jesus!"

They all laughed and said, "Yes, thank you Jesus!"

I asked him if he really thought he was O.K. could we just drive him? He agreed.

We got to the emergency room and they got us back there pretty quickly. After X-rays, the doctors astonishingly said he was clear to go. They did advise us that he was going to be very sore for a while and gave him crutches to use because he couldn't walk. To this day, every now and then he has some pain in his legs. But that is it. Isn't God amazing? We have what we call a "Joshua Garden" with a large cross and rocks at the bottom. We write prayer requests or testimonies on the rocks in permanent marker as a memorial for what God has done. We placed the cut open muck boots with the date at the bottom of the cross.

The previous story reminds me of a situation my husband and I were in where one lady had lost control. She was in deep panic and it could have gotten us all killed. On May 3, 2015 two Jihadists attacked Curtis Culwell Center in Garland, TX, where a Draw Mohammed Contest was being held in support of Charlie Hebdo who was attacked and killed by Jihadists in France for drawing cartoons of Mohammed. Incidentally, not long before this event, Muslims held a "Stand with the Prophet" event at the same venue in Garland. I was at the event along with my husband and teammates working inside security. This is an inside view.

Upon entering the Curtis Culwell Center, security was of utmost tightness. There was a heavy presence of undercover agents (who weren't so undercover if you know what to look for) and a SWAT Team. They had several security checkpoints upon entering and no weapons were allowed inside. If your name wasn't on the list, you weren't getting in, unless you were with the media (a convenient way to slide your way into an event uninvited).

There were over 200 people in attendance, excluding the media and law enforcement. A peaceful, energetic atmosphere pervaded among the attendees. People came from all over the US and the world. Our main job was assisting with sales and media coverage of the event, to include live-streaming as well as watching for anything that didn't fit. A couple of our team members made several rounds outside along the perimeter, hoping to get some footage of the protestors. There was just one problem. There were absolutely no, none, zero protestors. (This was very odd). When they returned their exact words were, "It's eerily quiet out there." One of these guys is a former US Army Ranger, my husband. He knows what to look for before a fire fight goes down. In fact, he told me that is how they knew to expect counter-attacks and counter-fire; if the town was quiet and absent of residents, something was coming. If there were people present and going about their day, it was most likely that they would not receive any retaliation or fire.

The event went on smoothly. As it ended, people began gathering in the foyer, talking and buying things. All of the live stream equipment was still running. A few of the attendees had exited the building. Then it happened...two ISIS Jihadists opened fire on over 200 Americans in a "no-gun" zone. Thankfully, the only fatalities were the two Jihadists. I say that because in the midst of this crisis, we were whisked away into an interior safe room while the firefight raged outside. Once the situation was somewhat controlled they had coordinated several buses driven by SWAT members to pick us up. We had to go in waves and not all together, so we didn't become a target. When our turn came to load a bus, there was a lady who was in shock and panicking. She stood at the door of the building, yelling at us to get the pizza boxes. This doesn't seem like something one would be concerned about, considering we had just been attacked by terrorists. However, because she was in shock, she didn't know how to respond appropriately. She stood, stricken with fear, and unable to move toward the van. At this point, we were exposed to the outdoors and not sure if there were any more terrorists waiting to fire. Because this lady didn't remain calm, she caused everyone else to be exposed to danger. Finally, the husband grabbed her by the waist and carried her to the bus! We all quietly cheered him on. The buses speedily drove us in and out of obstacles and to our next safe place.

There may be times in a crisis situation where someone panics and becomes a danger to everyone else. Just know this, you may have to make the hard decision to contain that person. This may involve whatever it takes to get them quiet, like knocking them out. I am very serious. It all depends on the circumstances. This lady's screaming and hesitation not only drew attention to us, but it prolonged our exposure to possible attacks. Don't be that person! Remain calm. If you need to take a second to gather your composure, do it. But remain calm and do not become a hindrance or a danger to the rest of the group. It's unfortunate that we have to even discuss this, but in our day and age when mass shootings are on the rise and terrorist attacks are a real part of our culture, we have to know how to respond.

I share this next example to show you the importance of having everything in its place and remaining calm in a crisis. That is one of the very first things you and your family need to know, always stay calm. A crisis is not the time or place to lose your cool. During a crisis seconds count. You have no time to waste. Have emergency phone numbers handy where all family members can see them. Have emergency numbers listed in your "favorites" list on your cell phone. Know how to get to the emergency facilities in your area and know which ones are more capable of handling what types of situations. We know that one hospital has anti-venom on hand, while the other does not. Another hospital is more capable in handling burn injuries. It is also more equipped to handle pediatric patients. You want to know these things before a crisis, not find them out after. It was good that I not only knew where the burn gel was in this next example, but that it was actually in its place!

This next emergency also involves our son. (Those boys.) He was frying churros on the gas stove in our kitchen. The grease had gotten too hot too fast, and as he put a churro in, the grease exploded up to the ceiling, and all over his face. He jumped back and fell to the floor with his hands covering his face. He was laughing at first, and then started yelling, "This burns! It's really burning!" I called the emergency room asking what we should do while trying to get him to the hospital, since we lived more than forty-five minutes away. He was at the bathtub splashing cold water on his face. They told us that whatever we do not to put cold water on it. Yet, that is the only thing that made it feel better. He told me he was praying for God to take the pain away. As he held that cold wash cloth over his face, God took the pain away. He looked up and said, "Well, I guess I have another testimony coming!" Wow! That boy has the faith of a mustard seed. The burns were all over his face, eyelids, and lip. I knew it was bad.

The ER said on the phone they couldn't get him in, and the urgent care said they couldn't treat him. We drove to the ER anyway, praying the whole way and asking others to pray. We prayed for God to take his pain away and for there to be no scarring. Our son was very concerned about scarring. Well, he wanted one small scar for war stories. What boy wouldn't? He said he didn't feel any pain as long as he kept that cold wash cloth on his face. We walked in. The charge nurse took one look at him and ushered him back. My friend, Millie, was on her way. The doctor checked him out and said he had second and third degree burns and he was going to need to scrape them. He warned him that it was going to be very painful and they could give him an iPad to distract him while he did the procedure. My son turned it down; he's not much for video games and electronics. He also warned us, he would need to have a couple of skin grafts and they had already scheduled this procedure for Thursday, two days away.

Millie had arrived. We laid our hands on him and prayed over him while the doctor stepped out for about fifteen minutes. He had left to get the tools to scrape the burns. We prayed specifically that my son would not feel any pain during the procedure and the burns would heal without scarring.

Upon the doctor's arrival he looked at my son and asked, "Weren't there two burns on his left cheek?"

I told him, "Yes." ONE WAS GONE! Hallelujah! The doctor looked bewildered. He proceeded scraping the burns.

After he was done, he asked my son, "How was that?"

My son replied, "How was what?"

The doctor responded curiously, "The scraping? Wasn't that painful?"

My son responded, "Oh, I was waiting for you to start!"

Praise God! He didn't feel a thing! The doctor told us it would take at least two years for total healing and for most of the scarring to fade. He said we'd need to protect his face from the sun and put sun block on, even in the winter. For the next few weeks we needed to wash his burns and apply antiseptic burn gel twice a day and report two days later for the grafting.

Over the course of the next seven days we witnessed an awesome miracle. Within hours his face was already looking better. I took pictures every day, sometimes twice a day. I was in complete awe. By the seventh day our son's face was completely healed! There was NO evidence whatsoever of any burns. The second day his face had healed so much I called the Burn Unit to tell them we no longer needed the appointment. I explained to her how the burns looked and she agreed.

I've included pictures and the dates are below so you'll notice it happened on the 14th and the last picture is on the 22nd. We count seven days because the accident happened so close to midnight. The last picture was the ninth calendar day from the date of the accident. You can clearly see that when he woke-up on that day he was completely healed. Notice the first day and what a difference a couple of hours made. The most remarkable difference was on the 20th. Look at both pictures closely from that day. You can see on the 15th how puffy his eyelids were. Don't we serve a mighty God?!

 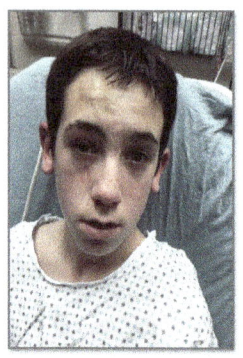 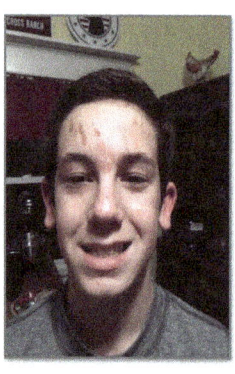

14MAR2017 8:55pm   14MAR2017 9:44pm   14MAR2017 11:57pm

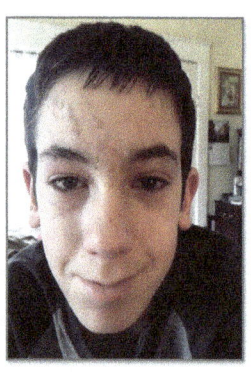  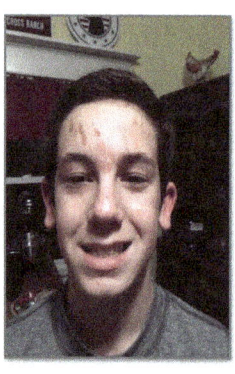

15MAR2017 10:07am   15MAR2017 11:02am   16MAR2017 9:16pm

18MAR2017 8:24pm   19MAR2017 1:04pm   20MAR2017 10:06am

20MAR2017 1:51pm   21MAR2017 11:29am   21MAR2017 8:24pm

Let's get back to preparing and training for emergencies. You can role play and act like you are experiencing symptoms of a heart attack. Explain the entire procedure beforehand, and then reiterate to your children you are only role-playing, and you are perfectly healthy and safe. Explain that role playing will help them to respond in case anything happens, and they can better help you or daddy. If they make mistakes, discuss it right away and show them the proper procedure. This is a great time to include those practice emergency phone calls. Thankfully we had been training in our home school lessons on emergency preparedness and response. Though they initially responded with fear, I was able to point them back to calmness by tasking them with jobs. This is important. Someone needs to take charge in a crisis. If you are that person, when you see someone spiraling into panic give them a job to do. This will usually help reel them back in. If you can see they are too far gone, assign someone else to remove them from the scene as this can cause panic for others, especially the victims. If there is no one else, tell them sternly to go to a specific place and wait.

Your children should know how to use a phone and effectively call for help. I would practice these calls with my children and have them call my dad or brother to go through practice rounds so they were familiar with how an emergency call would go. As soon as they are able, your children need to know their full name, who they should give that information to, and who they shouldn't. Do the same thing with their address and phone number. Make an index card with all of this pertinent information and then laminate it. This card is to remain with their backpack and needs to go with them any time they are separated from you.

When it comes to sleepovers, I highly encourage you to know the family and the home well if you are going to allow them. We did not allow our children to stay the night with friends until we felt they were mature enough to say, "No" to inappropriate things on television or online, etc. This would include inappropriate behavior from any of the family members within the home. They need to not only know when to say, "No" but have the courage to say, "No" if it is required. The goal is that they not ever be put in that situation to begin with. Before we would even allow our children to enter another home, we made sure one of us knew both parents well, along with any other family members in the home or friends of family members. We visited the home and checked it out. We would be upfront and let the parents know that we wouldn't allow our children in their home until we felt comfortable that they would be safe. We asked them if they keep alcohol in the home and if they do, do they have unsecured weapons in the home. There is nothing wrong with asking this. If they respond with defensiveness or anger, you should take that as a red flag and not allow your child to be in their home without you. This is for your child's safety.

When I was around six years old, I was allowed in my friends' homes because our families knew each other. What my parents didn't know was that one of the families would show horror films or "X" rated movies on the TV while we sat in the living room eating dinner. The siblings of the friend I was visiting often had parties where they would smoke pot and do drugs. I inhaled marijuana as a young child, watched teenagers make out, listened to inappropriate music. This was not uncommon for several of my friends' homes. At another friend's house, her parents let us stay home alone while we were in junior high school. We would venture into the alcohol cabinet and experiment. Several of my friends' parents had pornographic material readily available. My parents didn't know. I was not a Christian at the time, and I didn't have enough courage to tell my parents for fear of getting in trouble. Unfortunately, this had a very grave impact on me as a teenager and young adult. Please, protect your children. It is OK to ask tough questions. If the person gets offended, take that as a cue to move on and not allow your child to be at their home unattended.

Always have a back-up plan for your children in any case. If they feel uncomfortable for any reason, they should be able to call you and tell you they want to come home. Even if it's 2:00 am, go get them. Never let your child stay somewhere they don't feel comfortable. I would encourage you to not allow your young children to stay anywhere alone, without a sibling or you - even if it's family, unless you know them very well and are comfortable with their way of life. Too often child sexual abuse occurs from members of the family.

Teach them about stranger danger and how to know who they can trust. When in public, if they get lost, teach your children to find another mother who has children with her, as she is more likely to protect your child until someone safe arrives. They cannot always trust someone in uniform. Many places hire security guards that may look like law enforcement. These folks are not always the safest for your children. (Please see recommended reading list at the back of this book.) Protecting our children is an important aspect of family health, as well as teaching them how to recognize potential dangers.

      A subject that we must address is that of our own health and fitness. I thoroughly despise running unless a dog is chasing me, but let's face it, running is one of the quickest ways to a lean body. Ladies, if we want our husbands to maintain interest in us, we want to ensure that we are taking care of ourselves as best we can. Just because you've got that ring on your finger doesn't mean it's time to let yourself go; quite the opposite. There are plenty of women out there who will go to great lengths to get your married-with-a-ring-on-his finger husband's attention. I am not excusing adultery or saying that it is all up to you. What I am saying is, let's do everything within our power to prevent his eyes from even wanting to wander. Keep his interest focused on you. Do NOT get in the habit of putting yourself down in front of him. Do not complain about your weight or your looks to him. Look, he married you didn't he?

Don't you think there's something there that attracted him to you besides your witty personality? Trust me, you want to find a way to show confidence in yourself. This is very attractive to men. Most men are not drawn to a woman who has a low self-esteem. That usually causes them to run.

Find time in your day to exercise. If you don't enjoy running, find something else invigorating, such as hiking, cycling (They make amazing children strollers for bikes, no excuses), swimming, dancing, aerobics classes, etc. There are so many options that you have no excuses. I would strap my son in a baby carrier on my chest and hit the gym. If a gym is not in your budget you can purchase affordable items you can use in your home such as resistance bands, dumbbells, stability balls and all sorts of fun contraptions. The point is, get moving.

Pay attention to your diet. Don't allow yourself to fall into the trap of eating out of boredom or from emotion. Take control of your eating habits. A good rule of thumb is that you stop eating BEFORE you feel full. If you wait until after your stomach is hurting you have over eaten. Drink lots of water. Choose smaller portions. When you dine out consider placing half of your meal in a to-go box and eating it for another meal later on. Try to include fruits and vegetables with your meals. In fact, fruits and vegetables make a great snack between meals. Limit your sugar intake. Sugar is addictive. The more you eat the more you want it. It's like that chips commercial, "Bet you can't eat just one!" Sugar is the same way. I have read in many research articles that sugar is a cancer feeder. 1 Corinthians 6:19-20 says, "Or do you not know that your body is a temple of the Holy Spirit within you, whom you have from God? You are not your own, [20] for you were bought with a price. So glorify God in your body." We want to consider everything that we put into our bodies and whether it glorifies God or dishonors Him.

HOSPITALITY

I know I keep saying each subject is one of my favorites, but it's actually very true. I suppose I should just say that being a homemaker, being a housewife is my absolute favorite!

Hospitality is a gift. Not everyone carries the gift of hospitality, but everyone should know how to be hospitable. There are those who naturally know how to put a on a great gathering or party and there are those that could use a little help.

First Peter 4:9 tells us, "Show hospitality to one another without grumbling." That's pretty simple. What exactly does this mean? Hospitality without grumbling means your guests feel so welcomed in your home that they feel as though they are part of your family. You don't make them feel un-welcomed. This may be as simple as not looking at your watch or your phone. Engage in conversations. Ask your guests about themselves instead of constantly talking about yourself. Offer them drink and food. Make your home, their home. Let's dive in!

After reading the previous chapters, you should be ready for company. Having friends and family over is one of our favorite things. We enjoy spending time with our loved ones. If you have friends or family that are challenged in the area of overstaying their welcome, simply give specific times. You can say something like this "We would love to have you over for dinner and games from 6:00pm until 8:00pm." You set an end time.

If 8:00pm is approaching and no one appears to be preparing to leave, this is a great time to begin clean-up in the kitchen. This doesn't mean we ignore our guests, we simply begin cleaning up. This is usually a very effective method of ending a gathering, as most people don't care to join you in clean-up! Haha. Seriously though, some will and that is fine, but will definitely get the message across that the time is drawing near for guests to leave. Your private family time is precious. It must be protected. Remember, if guests don't want to leave, that is a compliment to you! They are enjoying themselves. It may be that you are perfectly fine with them hanging out until whenever, that is great too! Now, on to the fun stuff!

Hosting gatherings is a very important and fun ministry. That's right, ministry. First of all, if you have scriptures present on your walls and throughout the house, they're going to read that. This may be the only time they ever read scripture. Secondly, they will witness how you and your family carry yourselves and see how you treat one another as well as your graciousness toward them. This is a perfect opportunity to be a walking testimony of the love of Jesus. Take advantage of it.

If you follow the advice in the previous chapters, your home should be fairly clean. But before company arrives, do a once over with the dust rag, vacuum cleaner, and mop. Mind you, after guests leave, you will most likely do this again. Not because your guests are dirty, but because you've had a lot of traffic through the house and people were likely eating and drinking in places other than the dining table. Some guests may not appreciate your "no shoes" rule if you decide to implement that. Nonetheless, you want your home clean and presentable. This isn't because you are trying to impress others; rather you desire that your guests feel comfortable in your home. Visiting someone's home and sitting on a sofa that is overcrowded with dirty or clean laundry is uncomfortable. It is not very appetizing to show up for dinner at someone's house and they have dirty dishes piled up in the sink and on the counter.

The idea is to treat your guests like royalty. Their experience at your home should be a memorable one, for good reasons. It is good for them to feel loved and experience the presence of the Lord. When guests are over, that is not the time to have a family disagreement. Turn off your television when guests come over unless you invited them over to watch a game or a movie. Your guests should feel as though they are the center of the gathering. If you are hosting a party with multiple guests, make every effort to socialize with each one on a personal level, but keep it to a minimum so the other guests don't feel left out.

When it comes to children visiting your home, remember that it is your home and it is all right to set rules and standards for young company. We never allow our children to eat anywhere else except the dining table, and we don't allow them to walk, stand, or jump on our furniture. When we have young children visit that don't follow these standards, I gently make them aware of our rules. If they continue to disregard these rules, I address the parents. (Yes, there were numerous times the parents allowed their children to run amuck in our home, even after I told them our rules.) If the parents refuse to do anything about it, I occasionally have to pick the child up, set them on the floor, get down on their level, and politely explain the reason behind the rules. If they continue to disregard our rules, they have to take a seat at the table. The parents usually step in at his point and punish the children for misbehaving. Use this opportunity to minister to the parents in a loving way and show them how children are expected to obey and behave. If this is something you are not comfortable with, I totally understand. And it may be a good opportunity to set a childrearing book on the coffee table. (Wink, wink).

COOKING

One of my favorite topics is cooking! More accurately, one of my favorite activities is cooking. It is quite therapeutic. I enjoy every aspect of it - meal planning, prepping, cooking and serving.

    I have great childhood memories of my mom cooking in the kitchen. In my later childhood years, I recall my dad in the kitchen more too. I loved the aromas and watching them take a bunch of amazing ingredients, throw them together, and create art!

I enjoyed the fellowship aspect just as much. It is no wonder that I greatly enjoy cooking with my children today. Cooking is serving. When you cook a meal for others you are serving them. Food brings people together. Food brings comfort and conversation. Food brings healing.

I encourage you to teach your children how to cook while they're young. When my children were toddlers, I began letting them get their own breakfast. They could get cereal with milk or make toast or get some fruit. Some of my family members thought this was not a good idea and they were too young and needed help. What they didn't see was that I was helping them learn that they are not incapable of getting their own food and that when they make a mess, they can clean it up. I was helping them learn how to recover from a mistake. This is a huge lesson learned in a small and safe way. Obviously, I wasn't letting them handle butcher knives at age two, but they were allowed to prepare minor meals.

As our children got older, their responsibilities and privileges increased. Once they were able to safely handle a knife, they learned how to chop and cut vegetables. When they knew better than to touch the stove top, they began learning how to use the stove. When our youngest was around eight years old, I began having them each prepare, cook and serve a main course meal once a week. They each learned how to prepare breakfast, lunch and dinner with a dessert, and how to balance meals for nutrition. Everything they made had to be from scratch and not from a box. During these lessons, they learned the importance of nutrition and how God provides great foods, spices, and herbs for us and how they can bring healing to our bodies and prevent many illnesses. We also grew a lot of our own spices, vegetables and herbs which created an intense interest and desire to use what they had grown. They felt like they played a big role in the meal. They also learned how to set a table properly, yes, there is a proper way. I highly encourage you to research table etiquette as well as general etiquette lessons for your children, both boys and girls. This is a lost and dying art.

Cooking can and should be a lot of fun when viewed with the right heart posture. Dining together and meals are often mentioned throughout scripture. Acts 2:46 shows us the importance of breaking bread together (sharing a meal), "Day by day continuing with one mind in the temple, and breaking bread from house to house, they were taking their meals together with gladness and sincerity of heart." There are many more scriptures that discuss the importance of breaking bread together. Around the family dinner table, we hear about our children's day or learn more about their characters and personalities. When we sit down for meals with one another, all phones and electronic devices should be put away and turned off. Our attention should be focused on those in front of us. Let us get better at doing relationships.

Back to food. Cooking and family health go hand-in-hand. When our children were babies through their early childhood years, we greatly limited their sugar intake and did not allow them to have soda. It has been proven how terrible soft drinks are for teeth, especially baby teeth. Sugar has the same effect. We never really allowed them to have candy or candy bars until they were around ten or so. You should have seen their eyes the first time I let them pick out a candy bar. They had no idea what anything was. We never had tons of junk food sitting around. We mostly had homemade food and treats that were healthy (usually).

As I have said before, food brings people together and it has a way of bringing comfort. That being said, we do not want to allow food to become an addiction or an idol, so we must learn to control our temptations and our desire. I have found that keeping a stocked supply of healthy treats such as nuts, pretzels, dried fruits, healthy crackers, vegetables, fruits, dark chocolate covered nuts, and cheese is a great way to stave off those hunger pangs until dinner. I began having an "anytime" snack drawer in the fridge that had yogurt, cheese, fruits, veggies, etc. that the children could go to anytime they wanted without asking. This helped them feel like they were making more decisions, but they were decisions I was OK with. Of course they weren't allowed to just sit and consume a ridiculous amount at one time.

Whenever possible, I use the most natural and best ingredients available, even if it costs a little more money. Our family prefers to use organic, non-GMO, non-hormone, non-antibiotic ingredients. There is a lot of controversy around this topic, and I am not looking to debate it or persuade one group to believe a different way. I am just sharing my choices after doing my own research. Using natural foods is a much healthier option. Let's face it, there are so many ingredients being put into our food these days and we wonder why there are so many illnesses and allergies. I am willing to pay more for healthier foods for my family. We try to stay away from processed foods as much as we can and avoid the processed food aisle at the store, with the exception of the cereal aisle. With regard to cereal, we choose the healthier, more natural options. Grape Nuts is a great choice. We typically do not stock soda or candy in our home. We do not have alcohol in our home. Let me share what we do keep on hand though!

    Let's talk milk! We are so grateful for a local creamery that still sells milk in glass jugs. We are able to return the empty, clean jugs for a rebate. After the rebate, the milk is honestly, more affordable than the other junk. Organic milk is still not the same as fresh, all-natural, unpasteurized, cream milk. The cream milk literally has a layer of cream at the top. This is the good stuff ya'll! Add a little dollop of this cream to your coffee, oh my! This is the only milk we use in our home. And it is the only milk I use in baking, especially for customers. The nutrients in this whole, fresh, all-natural, cream milk are too great to bypass. We have not used skim milk or even 2% in our home in a very long time. If for some reason the cream line milk is not available, we resort to fresh whole milk. We have never had any issues using this milk. In fact, we are quite a healthy family.

For butter we use Kerrygold, which is a grass-fed, all-natural butter product. It is real butter. I use unsalted for baking and salted for cooking. We keep our salted butter out on the counter in a butter dish, as they do in Europe. When we were raising our own chickens, we kept our eggs out as well. If you raise your own chickens, don't wash the eggs until ready for use. The natural protective layer, called a bloom, protects the inside from any bacteria contaminating the egg. We recently sold our chicken stock and started buying eggs from the store after moving closer to city limits. We buy eggs that are pastured, uncaged, free-range and on all-natural, non-GMO, non-hormone/antibiotic feed. The way you can tell the difference is in their yolks. A healthy egg yolk will have a very deep, orange-yellow, almost burnt orange yolk. The white of the egg will be clear and not milky or creamy. This is a healthy egg.

We use unbleached flour because there is less processing in it. It is more wholesome. It also aids in richer baked products, such as cakes and cookies. The same is true for sugar.

When it comes to olive oil, choose a high quality brand. This is not something you want to skimp on. The quality of olive oil you use determines the outcome of your food. Go big!

Salt! I only buy and use pink Himalayan sea salt. I order salt from San Francisco Salt Company. They also produce deliciously flavored salts. It is believed that sea salt is much healthier for you. Regular table salt tends to be higher in sodium; however, because of its natural harvesting process pink Himalayan sea salt contains more calcium, potassium, magnesium, and iron. It is believed that sea salt can improve respiratory diseases, balance the body's pH, reduce signs of aging, improve sleep quality, regulate blood sugar and increase libido. The taste also makes an amazing difference in your baked products. A little goes a long way though. You do not need to use nearly as much sea salt as you do idolized salt. You will not want to go back after using this.

Herbs and spices are a super fun and healthy way to jazz up any recipe. I often use fresh herbs and spices rather than dried; however, there is nothing wrong with dried. Fresh herbs and spices seem to be a little bolder, requiring less than a dried measurement. We grow several spices, so we have access to fresh ones. We grow lots of oregano because it is great in food but it can also add a pleasant aroma to any flower arrangement. Rosemary is a good medicinal herb. We grow basil, thyme, oregano and mint. Mint, along with lime added to tea is so delicious. Lavender is a great addition to floral arrangements. I often put lavender with rosemary and thyme in a sweet little vase to brighten up a room and give it a nice aromatic touch.

Spices to keep in the cupboard:

Garlic salt
Garlic powder
Onion powder
Minced onion
Italian seasoning
Oregano
Basil
Thyme
Rosemary
Sage
Parsley
Cumin
Turmeric
All Spice
Paprika

Celery, crushed
Dill
Celery
Cayenne pepper
Chili pepper
Lemon pepper
Ground ginger
Ground clove
Whole cloves
Ground nutmeg
Cinnamon sticks
Ground cinnamon
Crushed black pepper
Meat seasoning
Meat tenderizer

Kitchen Staples:

Kitchen Aid Mixer
Large stock pot
Good set of kitchen knives
Measuring bowls, cups and spoons
Unbleached flour
Whole wheat flour
Bread flour
All-natural, whole, pure cane sugar
Brown sugar
Powdered sugar
Vanilla (The good kind, not imitation)
Variety of flavorings such as almond
Baking soda
Baking powder
Rice
Tapioca
Quality olive oil
Quality coconut oil
Quality vegetable oil
Powdered egg whites for emergencies
Evaporated milk
Sweetened condensed milk
Himalayan sea salt
Black pepper
Shortening
All-natural, grass-fed, unsalted butter
All-natural, grasped salted butter
Worcester sauce
Browning Sauce
Marsala cooking wine
Canned cream of chicken
Chicken bouillon cubes
Beef bouillon cubes

When I cook, I include herbs and spices that bring nutritional value to our bodies. Garlic is almost always included, and it's almost always fresh. I use a lot of garlic in my recipes, meaning I use it often and I use a lot of it. So, get happy with it! Garlic is great for heart health, immunity, toothaches, allergies, joint and digestive health; it's a cancer fighter, and so much more. You can't go wrong with garlic. Onion and many pepper varieties provide the same benefits. Turmeric is excellent for brain health, joint and cardiovascular health.

When you prepare a meal, always incorporate lean meat, which includes certain varieties of fish, seafood and typically any white meat. When I cook with red meat, I use the leanest cuts or ground I can find. Include at least one vegetable and one fruit. Use healthy grains such as whole wheat, multi-grains, wild rice, quinoa, oats, etc. Typically, the healthiest way to serve fruits and vegetables is in raw form. Next, would be to grill, smoke, bake, or boil. The least healthy way is frying.

Before you cook, plan your meal from start to finish. Know exactly what ingredients you will need and to give yourself enough time to make a grocery run if necessary. Once you have your ingredients and supplies, begin prepping your workspace. This includes sanitizing your countertops and your hands as well as tying up your hair and removing any loose strands from your clothing.

Make sure your cutting knives are sharpened. Dull knives are dangerous and laborious. Read all instructions prior to beginning so you can time everything correctly. You want to avoid having one dish ready an hour before everything else, as this can cause it to get tough, unpleasant looking, or dried out.

It is usually suitable to prepare other dishes early but not actually cook them until such a time that allows everything to be ready simultaneously. If you are making homemade breads or anything that requires rising, plan ahead to allow enough time for the rising process. One way to help speed it along is to boil a pot of water and place it in an enclosed space, such as a laundry room or even the oven. Just remember you put it in there before turning on the oven! (Yes, said from experience.) Make your dough first thing in the morning. The great thing about dough rising is that you can't really over-rise it (Unless you're Lucy Ricardo - a character form the *I Love the Lucy Show*.)

As mentioned in the "Cleanliness" chapter, I like to clean as I go, so I have less work after the meal. This also creates a safer cooking environment. While aprons may seem out of style, they are very helpful in protecting our clothes from hard-to-remove stains. There are many styles and affordable aprons available. If you are going to spend a lot of time in the kitchen (which I secretly hope you do!), you may want to invest in some house shoes that provide good foot support or purchase a supportive mat to place in front of the sink and the stove.

Always remember that when cooking, slower is better. Never rush anything. This can create a disaster real quick. You can always cook something longer, but you can never un-cook anything. There are those rare recipes that call for fast or super hot cooking, but in general, slower is better. If you find that what you are cooking is getting dried out, you can usually add a softening agent such as water, oil, butter, or juice. I normally use a non-stick spray, oil or butter to pre-grease my dishes so that clean up is easier.

When making thick sauces or creams, thicken them with flour, cornstarch, or tomato paste. If your sauce or cream is not thick enough, don't panic. You can fix that! Get a small glass or measuring cup and add 1-3 tablespoons of flour or any thickening agent mentioned previously. Add very cold water, then stir it well, eliminating any chunks or globs. Once you have created a thick paste, pour it slowly into your sauce or cream and mix well. If you your sauce or cream is too thick you can simply add a little water, oil, broth, cream, milk, or juice. Go slow though and give it time to heat up before adding too much. The heat assists in thickening. You will gain more experience and wisdom over time. Just remember, almost anything is correctable except over cooking. Go slowly.

When baking cookies or cheesecakes you will see some cracking on the top begin to take place, this is a good indicator that they are ready to come out, that is, if you desire chewier cookies. If your cake or bread still has the consistency of Jell-O in the center, it is probably too early to come out of the oven. If you notice your cake, bread or pie beginning to brown around the edges you can place foil over the top or just the edges. This will prevent it from burning. Once you can push your finger in the center and it springs back, it is ready to pull out. Let it cool completely before trying to remove from the pan. Otherwise you may find yourself trying to piece it together like a puzzle.

Rice and pasta are an essential part of many meals. There is a proper way to cook them. Both are things you want to avoid overcooking. Overcooked rice and pasta become sticky and sometimes mushy, causing it to fall apart. If you under cook either they are hard and tough. If you can cut the pasta in half easily with a spoon it is ready. It should appear limp but not sticky. Once your pasta is ready, add a tablespoon of olive oil to it to keep it from getting sticky and to keep it fresh longer. This is especially good for leftover pasta. For the rice you want to add about a tablespoon of butter for every cup of rice. I like to add dill to our rice. It gives a nice, light flavor. When reheating rice it is often better to add a little water and reheat it over the stove.

Making bread and other dough is very similar to creating thick sauces or creams. If you find that your dough is too sticky, it needs a little more flour or whatever grain you are baking with. If it is too dry and crumbly, add liquid a little at time. Use the original liquid from the beginning of the recipe. Cookies are the same way. If your dough is too sticky add flour. If it is too dry and difficult to work with, add a very tiny amount of milk or oil. Another thing you can try is refrigerating the dough for about an hour. This can often aid in making the dough more manageable.

This is probably a good time for me to tell you that when baking you want to follow the recipe exactly when it comes to rising agents (baking soda, baking powder, and salt) until you have enough experience to know if and when you can add a little more. When it comes to flour you most likely need to stick pretty closely to the recipe. As for sugar and vanilla…get happy with it!

One of the most important things I want to share with you is to get creative! Use the recipe as a base until you get good at it. Then, let your creative juices flow. As you learn what various herbs and spices tastes like, you will discover which ones are your favorite and which ones are not. You'll also learn this about your family too. If a recipe simply calls for salt and pepper, why not add garlic, onion, and thyme? Play around with flavors and experiment. This makes cooking so much more enjoyable. Again, just like you can't un-cook anything, you can't really reverse the amount of what you put in, so pour slowly.

The other area you can get creative in is presentation. Own your art! The actual cooking process is a lot of fun, but serving can be too. Create lovely displays with the final product. A great way to garnish, or dress-up a dish is adding a sprig of fresh rosemary, thyme, oregano, basil or mint. You can also use wedges of lemon, lime or orange. Or drizzle Worcester sauce or dressings over a meat or vegetable dish.

Cooking is an art and can be a lot of fun. The right perspective means everything. Just like housekeeping, cooking is a ministry. We will not only cook for our families but for others as well. When you become a good cook, you can serve others and minister to them through food. Much conversation occurs over a good meal. You may have a girlfriend that really needs someone to minister to her and disciple her. Bake something delicious, put on a pot of coffee and invite her over. This setting opens doors for intimate conversation where her heart can feel safe and the Lord can minister to her through you. Don't view cooking as just another chore.

See cooking as a ministry, not just to your family, but to so many others. Any time a new neighbor moves into the neighborhood I will bring them freshly baked bread or cookies and a note of encouragement along with our phone number. It has often been said that, "Food is the way to a man's heart." I'd like to suggest that it's not just to a man's heart but any person's heart. Who doesn't enjoy good food?

FAVORITE RECIPES

I am super excited about this chapter! Cooking and baking are two of my favorite therapies and hobbies. I cannot say enough about the significance of putting together a great meal. There is an art to it really. The presentation is crucial, but the taste is even more important. Learning about proper nutrition and what vegetables compliment main course dishes is key. It is a science in addition to being an art. We want our families to be as healthy as possible and home cooking

is the better option compared to frozen and processed meals.

When it comes to baking desserts, I get really happy with vanilla, sugar, and spices such as cinnamon, cloves, ginger, nutmeg and cardamom. Sugar and vanilla especially, add pure enjoyment to any dessert! Get happy with it! Just remember, vanilla is a liquid and may alter the consistency of your recipe, so you may need to tweak the grain ingredients such as sugar or flour. These will help to balance out the liquid vs. solid ingredients and maintain the correct consistency. What I mean is this: If you add too much vanilla and not enough flour to your cookies, they may end up runny and skimpy. You simply add a little bit of flour until you have the sturdier consistency a cookie needs. If you have added too much sugar, simply add a drop or two of vanilla.

Now, for the recipes! Proceed with caution and excitement! I very rarely measure anything, unless I am baking, even then…it's loose measuring. I have learned throughout the years how much is enough of any one ingredient. This comes with experience, time, and preference. So, while I may list a measurement with some things, it is a loose measurement unless stated otherwise. In most cases, especially with meal preparation, you will simply see an ingredient listed. When there is no measurement listed it is up to you how much to use, or if you will use it at all.

When using vegetables or fruits in cooking or baking you want to go with fresh. If that is not an option, then frozen or canned.

When it comes to cooking, be patient. You never want to rush anything to bake or cook. What I mean by this is that you want to avoid increasing temperatures to hurry something along. Slower cooking is usually best, with a few exceptions. This goes for cooking meals or baking. You may wonder what the difference is between cooking and baking. When I refer to baking, I am referring to using grains, sugars, risers, etc. and most often finishing the product in an oven. Cooking is the preparation of main course meals and side dishes.

Another note; electric versus gas…always go with gas if you have the opportunity. Gas convection ovens and ranges are the best for your cooking experience and pleasure. It delivers a great product with even cooking. Now, for the fun part!

Gumbo

(My favorite, my late Grandma Lena Saladino taught me this recipe, I tweaked it a little)

Ingredients:

Large stock pot (Gumbo)

2 Medium pots (ochre and broth)

1 large pot (rice)

Authentic, high grade olive oil (Don't go cheap on your oils)

Hot Damn (Found on the spice isle)

Lobster Base

Marsala Cooking Wine (Make this a staple)

Chicken bouillon cubes

Browning Sauce

Unbleached Flour

Frozen ochre 2-3 bags (One of the only times I use frozen anything)

1 large white onion, chopped

Chives, chopped

Cloves of garlic, chopped (As much as your heart desires! I typically use the whole foot.)

Several celery stalks, chopped

Green pepper, chopped

2 Cans tomatoes diced with juices

4 Cans lump white crab meat

Fresh Gulf shrimp, peeled and deveined (If not available, frozen.)

Fresh crab legs

Italian seasoning

Turmeric

Dill

Oregano

Basil

Garlic Salt

Onion powder

Thyme

Sage

Rice

First, chop your vegetables. Cover the bottom of the pot with oil. Tenderize vegetables in the oil with some flour (To thicken to your liking.) Meanwhile, cook the ochre in a separate pot, strain the strings, set aside. In a third pot cook about 4-8 cups of rice depending on how many you're feeding when it's time to serve. In a fourth pot boil some water with chicken bouillon cubes, about 6-8 cups. Once the vegetables are tender, throw in the shrimp just to pink it up. Then add the boiling chicken broth, canned tomatoes, canned crab meat and all of the other ingredients. Put the crab legs in. Bring to a gentle boil, then, simmer with lid slightly covering for several hours. Gumbo is always best the second and third day as it kind of marinates itself sitting in the fridge.

Serve the gumbo over rice and homemade French herb bread or olive focaccia bread.

Crayfish Etoufee
(My son's favorite)

Ingredients:
Large stock pot (You might want to invest in a good one of these)
Olive oil
Marsala cooking wine
Lobster base
Unbleached flour
4-6 packages of frozen crayfish unless you can find it fresh.
4 Cans white lump crab meat
4 Cans Rotel with cilantro and lime
1 Can tomato paste, organic
2 Cans tomatoes diced, organic
1 Large, white onion chopped
1 Foot of garlic chopped (A foot is an entire grouping of cloves, or a head)
Chives chopped
3 Stalks celery chopped
Chili powder
Turmeric
Italian seasoning
Paprika

All Spice
Garlic Salt
Onion powder
Rice 4-6 cups

Tenderize vegetables in oil. Add crawfish and crabmeat and cook through. Add all the other ingredients and bring to a gentle boil, then simmer for several hours. Cook your rice. Again, this is great the second and third day. This one is delicious served up with homemade French herb bread or olive focaccia.

Jambalaya

Ingredients:
Large stock pot
2-4 lbs uncooked, peeled, and deveined shrimp or crayfish
Olive oil
Hot Damn
Lobster base
Unbleached flour 2-4 tbsp
Browning sauce 1/4 to 1/2 tsp
1 c ham chopped or cubed
1 green bell pepper chopped
1 jalapeño pepper (seeded if you prefer less kick) chopped
1 white onion chopped
1 foot or clump of garlic chopped
1 bay leaf
Thyme
Parsley
Sea salt
Black pepper
2-4 cans diced tomatoes
1-2 cans tomato sauce
2-4 c rice cooked

You will first cover the bottom of the stock pot with olive oil, then chop all your vegetables and tenderize with the flour. Add the raw shrimp or crayfish and cook until pink. Add the lobster base and the rest of the ingredients minus the rice. Cook the rice separately. Serve with salad and a sourdough bread or garlic bread.

Coconut Shrimp Soup

One of my personal favorites. This one was created one day when I hadn't been to the grocery and was limited on ingredients. I was in love with this soup at once!

Ingredients:
Large stock pot
Olive oil
Marsala cooking wine, about 1c
Heavy cream
Lobster base (A very tiny bit, maybe about 2-3 tsp)
Shrimp (or crayfish) uncooked, peeled, and deveined
Chicken broth or bouillon
1 white onion chopped or thinly sliced
4-6 garlic cloves chopped
2 stalks celery finely chopped
Lemon grass chopped
1 package Portabella mushrooms chopped or sliced
1/2 c shredded coconut
1-2 tbsp fresh cilantro chopped

Fresh-rosemary, thyme, basil, and dill finely chopped
A sprinkle of ground turmeric, chili powder and a dash of cardamom

Cover the bottom of the pot with olive oil and tenderize all the vegetables with flour. Add the uncooked shrimp or crayfish and cook until pink. Add the lobster base and heavy cream and cook at medium heat until thickened. Add the Marsala and all the seasonings, stirring frequently. Then add the broth. Bring to a gentle boil, then, simmer for several hours.

Shrimp Hoagies

Ingredients:

10-12 oz bag of frozen, cooked or fresh, peeled, and deveined shrimp.
2 lg ripe avocados
1/2 c shredded carrots or slaw
1/3 c bottled coleslaw dressing or tartar sauce
1 tsp Italian seasoning
Garlic salt
Onion powder
Ground turmeric
Dill, ground
Thyme, ground
Hoagie buns hollowed out.

Combine all of the ingredients except the bread. Mix well. Hollow out the buns and add the salad. I enjoy spreading some mayonnaise on my bread first. Serve with fresh salad and/or fruit.

Chicken or Turkey Tortilla Soup
(Everyone enjoys this one!)

Ingredients:
Large stock pot
Medium pot (broth)

Olive oil

Large white onion, chopped
Chives, chopped
A foot or 8-12 cloves garlic chopped
4-6 celery stalks chopped

1 Can corn drained
1 Can black beans, unseasoned
(You can add practically any vegetable you like)
4 Cans Rotel with cilantro and lime

4 packages of all-natural, organic chicken strips or leftover turkey from Thanksgiving

Garlic salt
Onion powder

Chile powder
Ground cumin (a lot)
Fajita season (liberal amount)
Thyme
Rosemary
Sage
Dill
Turmeric
Chopped Celery Seed

Fresh cilantro
Fresh avocado
Tortilla strips

Cover two glass pans with oil, put the washed chicken strips in them. Cover with the herbs and spices. (Leave them out, you'll use them again.) Bake at a very low temperature until cooked through and very tender. (250-275 degrees).

While the chicken is baking tenderize the vegetables over oil in the stock pot and begin boiling the bouillon cubes in 4-6 cups of water.

Once the chicken is finished put it in the stock pot with some of the juices from the pans. Add all the other ingredients, including a second round of spices and herbs. Bring to a gentle boil, then simmer for several hours. Like the Gumbo, this soup is delicious the second and third days also.

Garlic Infused Pot Roast Beef or Pork
(Another from Grandma Lena)

Ingredients:
1 medium to large slow cooker or Crockpot
1 pot roast (beef or pork) (Rump, shoulder is fine as well)
Olive oil
Marsala cooking wine
1 foot or clump of garlic (if it's small, then use two) half chopped the other half cut into spears for infusion in the roast
1 yellow onion sliced in quarters
3-5 stalks of celery sliced crossways
Sea salt
Black pepper
Garlic salt
Onion powder
Rosemary
Thyme
Sage
1-4 tbsp unbleached flour
2 chicken or beef bouillon cubes (Beef for beef roast, chicken for pork)
2-4 cups boiled water for bouillon

Preparation:

Wash the meat, as with any meat, before cooking it. Clean the area with bleach afterward.

Cover the bottom of the slow cooker with olive oil.

Place the meat in the slow cooker. Cut half of the garlic into spears and then with a sharp knife cut slits in the meat all over and push the spears of garlic into them. Brown all sides of the meat. Once this is complete, cover the meat with flour and the rest of the herbs and spices. Cut up the rest of the vegetables and place them in the pot. Add approximately one half to a whole bottle of Marsala. Meanwhile, boil the water and add the bouillon cubes. Once it has come to a rolling boil add to the pot.

Cook on high for about 1 hour and then adjust the temperature to medium or warm and maintain this for approximately 4-5 hours, or until cooked. This is a cut of meat that is ok to be somewhat undercooked as long as there are not pink juices flowing.

Serve with garlic mashed potatoes and/or homemade biscuits or rolls, potatoes and a green vegetable.

Spaghetti with Meat Sauce

Large stock pot
Olive oil
1-2 lbs ground beef browned with onions and garlic
1 white onion chopped
1 foot (clump) garlic chopped
1-2 cinnamon sticks
Cloves, ground, a pinch or more
Nutmeg, ground, a pinch
Italian seasoning
Oregano
Basil
Black pepper
Sea salt
Sugar
2-4 cans diced tomatoes
2-4 cans tomato sauce
Whole grain spaghetti pasta

Brown your meat with the chopped onions and garlic. Drain the grease. Add all of the other ingredients. Bring to a gentle boil, then simmer for 1-2 hours. Serve with homemade garlic French bread or olive focaccia bread and dinner salad.

Pizza
(A Popular Favorite)

(A highly sought after recipe, for the first time ever, made public)

Ingredients:
The first thing you need to know is that once you get the base ingredients you can and should be as creative as your heart desires. Play around with this one and experiment!

Crust:
1 tbsp dry yeast
1 1/2 c warm water
1-2 tbsp olive oil
Italian seasoning (I use a lot)
Oregano
Garlic salt (I use quite a bit) Minced onion 1-2 tbsp
Ground turmeric

4-5 c unbleached flour

Sauce:
1 can tomato sauce
1 tbsp olive oil
Italian seasoning
Oregano
Ground turmeric
Garlic salt
Minced onion
Sea salt
Black pepper

Toppings:
Other than shredded mozzarella or shredded fiesta blend cheese, the sky is the limit!
Pepperoni
Canadian bacon
Bacon pieces
Italian sausage
Chicken chunks
Pineapple
Mushrooms
Onions
Peppers

Anchovies (gross)
Tomatoes
Garlic, roasted
Goat cheese
Smoked Gouda cheese
Blue cheese

In a large measuring or mixing bowl mix the yeast with warm water until it's completely dissolved. Add 1 tbsp olive oil and the rest of the ingredients except the flour. Mix well. Stir in the flour, 1 cup at a time, mixing it well. When it gets too difficult to stir with a spoon begin to knead with your hands on a lightly floured surface, continuing to add the rest of the flour. You want a stretchy, elastic-like consistency in the dough. In a large bowl sprayed with non-stick spray or covered with oil, roll the dough to cover all sides and then cover the bowl with a cheesecloth or towel. If you live in an area where the humidity is low you can boil a small pot of water and place it in the oven with it turned off, and place the bowl of covered dough next to it and close the door. I will often place my rising dough in the laundry room while the dryer is running. This helps it to rise. While your dough is resting make the sauce.

Mix the ingredients for the sauce well, let stand. Cut up any vegetables you will be using and prepare the rest of your toppings.

Once your dough has risen to about twice its size, take it out of the bowl and place it on a lightly floured surface. Punch the ball of dough down with your fists into a circular shape. Roll it up into a log and then equally separate into four sections and roll those into balls. Cover with the towel and let rest for  about 20 mins. Take one ball and punch it down into a circle. Roll it out with a rolling pin or punch it down into the size you want it and place it on a pizza pan. I use either stoneware or pans with holes in them for a crisper crust, which we prefer. You can make your crust as thick or as thin as you like. If you choose thicker crust you may only have enough to make three pizzas. I can usually pull out 4-5 pizzas with thin crust.

Spread lightly (or more if you prefer more sauce) over the dough on the pan. Sprinkle with the cheese you desire. Top with toppings. An alternative to the tomato based sauce is sprinkling the dough with a little olive oil or even Alfredo sauce. Seriously, get creative with this, get happy about it!

Bake your pizzas on the lower rack for a crispier crust at 425° until it is golden on top and the cheese is completely melted. For a softer crust, place on the middle racks. If you desire stuffed crust allow for more dough at the edges and then pour cheese sauce around the perimeter and then seal with the excess dough.

You can serve your pizzas with garden salad and pecan praline cheesecake makes a great complimentary dessert.

Green Beans in Bacon Gravy

Ingredients:
Medium to large pot
4 cans green beans (2 drained) or 2 bags fresh green beans (cut the tips)
4-6 strips raw bacon
1-3 tbsp flour
Browning sauce
Worcestershire sauce
2-4 tbsp salted butter
Garlic salt
Minced onion
Sea salt
Pepper

Fry the bacon in the pan until crispy. Remove the bacon and immediately add the flour, minced onion, browning sauce and Worcestershire sauce with the butter. Stir frequently. Add the green beans, using the juice of two of the cans of green beans. If you are using fresh green beans you may want to add half a can of water. Cook through. Top with crumbled bacon.

Asparagus in Ginger Sauce

2 stalks of fresh asparagus (Cut the raw ends)
4-6 tbsp salted butter
2-4 tbsp Worcester sauce
Garlic salt
Onion powder
Chopped fresh ginger or ground ginger
Brown sugar

Cut the asparagus into 2 inch lengths
Put all the ingredients in a large pot on the stove and cook at medium heat until tender.

Garlic Mashed Potatoes

Ingredients:
6-8 large Idaho potatoes
4-6 tbsp salted butter
1 c sour cream
1-2 c whole milk
6-8 roasted garlic cloves
Onion powder
Sea salt
Black pepper

Chop your garlic cloves and place in a foil pouch with salted butter.

Peel your potatoes and quarter them, boil in a large pot of water until soft. Immediately drain the water and add all the above ingredients as you mash the potatoes with a potato masher or a pastry blender. Serve warm.

French Herb Bread

For this recipe and several others, I simply follow the Better Homes and Gardens New Cook Book, 11th Edition recipe for French bread. However, I add my personal touches to them. You follow the recipe exactly as it is in the cook book only add these ingredients to the dry mixture in the beginning:

Garlic salt
Onion powder
Thyme
Sage
Dill

I use a little more yeast than the recipe calls for. Once baking is complete I often cut the loaves in half long ways and spread garlic butter on the halves. You can make garlic butter by simply roasting some finely chopped garlic with butter in foil, in the oven.

Honey Cornbread

Ingredients:

4 boxes of Jiffy cornbread (This is one of the very few times I will use a packaged product. If I just really have a lot of time on my hands I will make the cornbread from scratch.)

4 eggs

1 $^{1/3}$ c milk

1 tbsp butter

4 tbsp raw, unfiltered honey

2 tbsp brown sugar

1 tsp chili powder

1 can creamed corn

You can add some thyme, rosemary, garlic salt, and onion powder to this recipe to give it some flavor.

Mix all the ingredients and pour into a baking dish. Bake at 400°. Cook until golden brown.

Cornbread Stuffing

Ingredients:

Using the recipe for the honey cornbread, bake your bread one to two days before you need to make the stuffing.

2-4 eggs beaten
2-5 celery stalks chopped
1 white onion chopped
4-6 toes of garlic chopped
1 green bell pepper chopped
1 red bell pepper chopped
1 jalapeño chopped
1-2 c chicken broth
Garlic salt
Onion powder
Thyme
Rosemary
Dill
Turmeric

Cumin

Let the cornbread sit out for a day or two and dry out. Crumble the bread into a large mixing bowl. Add all of the above ingredients and stir well. Pour into a baking dish and bake at 350° until golden brown.

Pumpkin Bread

Ingredients:

2c unbleached flour (use half in the beginning with dry ingredients, other half at the very end)

1c brown sugar, somewhat packed

A little more than 1 tbsp baking powder

1/2 tsp baking soda

1 1/2 tsp cinnamon

Dash of sea salt

Almost a 1/2 tsp nutmeg

Almost a 1/2 tsp ground cloves

Dash of cardamom

A little more than 1c pumpkin (fresh or canned)

1/2 c buttermilk (If you don't have buttermilk put 1tbsp lemon juice in regular milk and let sit for about 5 mins.)

1 tsp vanilla

2 eggs (free range, pastured eggs are best for baking)

1/3 c shortening

Mix all dry ingredients well with just 1c of the flour. Mix all the wet ingredients. Blend them together. Add the remaining flour and anything else that suits your fancy. I will often add walnuts and cranberries or white chocolate chips with cranberries. Pour batter into two separate bread pans. (I prefer using glass, it seems to cook more evenly). Bake at 350° until a toothpick comes out clean, or that you can see it has begun to crack at the top and when you shake it the Jell-O movement is gone.

Chewy Spiced Ginger Cookies

Ingredients:
3/4c shortening

1c pure cane sugar

1 egg

1/4c molasses

1/2 tsp vanilla

2c unbleached flour

1 tsp ground cinnamon

1 tsp ground ginger

1/2 tsp ground cloves

1/4 tsp cardamom

1 1/5 tsp baking soda

1/4 tsp sea salt

Cream the shortening and sugar in a mixer, until fluffy. Add the wet ingredients. Combine the dry ingredients separately, then, add to mixture. Mix well with a mixer. Roll into equal sized balls and roll in sugar. Place on an ungreased cookie pan and bake at 350° until they begin to crack on top and turn a light golden brown on the edges.

Pecan Praline Cheesecake

I initially follow the Cheesecake Supreme recipe in the Better Homes and Gardens New Cook Book, 11th Edition. But then, I get happy with it!

When making the crust I add about a tbsp of brown sugar. For the filling I add the following ingredients:

1 tbsp brown sugar
Dash of cardamom
1 tsp or so of cinnamon
1/2 tsp or so of ground cloves
1/2 tsp or so of nutmeg

I add another tsp of vanilla

For the topping I roast pecan halves in the oven at 300° until toasted, slightly brown and fragrant. Then, in a small sauce pan I melt:

1/2 c butter
1-2 tsp vanilla
1 tsp rum extract
2-3 tbsp brown sugar
10 pieces of caramel candy

I add the roasted pecans at the end and then serve this warm over cheesecake. This has an amazing, rich flavor. You will not disappoint your guests with this one. Play around with your own spices and extracts and see what you come up with!

MILITARY FAMILIES

As the wife of a US Army Ranger, military families have a place in my heart. Hero served for nearly nine years with one of the Ranger Battalions and another four years contracting overseas. He served on nine deployments between Iraq and Afghanistan. Too many of his comrades gave their lives in the war and too many funerals were attended. Many of our friends sustained serious combat wounds. My husband and many others sustained lifelong injuries. Military life never really ends for a family. It will always be part of you. It forever changes you.

One thing military life taught me is that life is precious and every second counts. Never waste an opportunity to be with your loved ones. Never leave a loved one without saying, "I love you." Always honor one another. Everyone handles things differently, and there's nothing wrong with that. Help each other cope through difficult times. Allow each other to cry.

Have a strong support system in place. I found our church family was the best place for my children and me, which included military families who shared a common faith. We did join some of the FRG (Family Readiness Group) events and made some good friends there. However, I was very particular who I chose to let close to our family. Unfortunately, military gatherings tend to include drinking, sometimes very heavy drinking. I wish this would change. It's a fact of military life that we have to approach wisely.

You learn very quickly who you can count on. You also find that military families are a unique brand. It is a brotherhood unlike any other. The closest thing I have seen to military brotherhood is the cowboy community. Your military family will not only be there as soon as you call, they will be there for you many years down the road. It's a family that never dissolves. There is such a common bond between military families that anywhere you go in the world, when you meet another military family, you instantly have a connection that binds you together.

I recall a time I was working a political event in Florida and Hero was deployed to Afghanistan. An Army Chinook was shot down in Wardak Province, Extortion 17. Thirty-eight men lost their lives, including a combat dog and handler. My husband was a K9 Handler at the time. During the event, my boss was speaking and received word of the shoot down. He shared the news with the conference attendees. My heart sunk and my mouth dropped. He then realized the connection. For the next fifteen minutes my phone was blowing up with messages from our FRG, friends, and family. So much miscommunication was coming in. We were told our husbands were involved. I was with a great political team at the time, which had many military connections. Within minutes, several Veterans had come to me with their concern. Two different military couples offered themselves however I needed. They did not leave my side. It was a very somber few hours of anxious anticipation. We finally received word of who exactly was involved. Then, I received the call…it was Hero's voice on the line. Praise God! He was safe. My point is this, absolute strangers, yet family, came to my aid. People whom I never met were at the ready to do whatever I needed. They offered to let me stay with them, fly me home, whatever was needed. Military families are family for life, whether you've ever met or not. Honor the brotherhood.

Invest time in your marriage, especially while he's home. This is a time to drop your plans with your girl friends and focus time on your husband. I didn't always do this well, and our relationship suffered for it. Your husband will likely want to get together with the guys from his team. While you may feel jealous about this, he needs time with his buddies, especially after returning from deployment. They have many experiences on their mind, things they may not want to share with their spouses. It won't be because he doesn't love you; rather, he may have experienced some extremely graphic and terribly difficult things while on missions and may feel the need to protect you from hearing the details. He may withhold certain things because he feels it will keep you from worrying while he's deployed the next time. However, he needs to be able to talk about these things. Chances are likely, several years down the road you will hear these stories and be so thankful he didn't share them back then. I encourage you to listen patiently and let him talk. Try not to ask too many questions and respect his experiences

During deployments host Bible studies and prayer groups. This was a huge asset to the wives in our group. These are the ladies I still keep in touch with. We met twice a week for Bible study and prayer. We met other days of the week just for fellowship and grocery runs. Meeting like this really helped the time go by faster. More importantly, it strengthened our faith and gave us peace while our husbands were in harm's way. Many prayers were answered right then, during our prayer meetings.

Once, a captain's wife had not heard from her husband in several weeks. Typically we lived by the rule, "No news is good news." However, things were pretty hot on this particular deployment and we had already lost several men. She was beginning to feel a little nervous about the lack of communication. We prayed for his safety and that she would receive confirmation soon that he was alright. Before we could finish praying he called her! Praise the Lord. Keeping the faith is vital for a military wife, so are the gatherings of wives. Don't neglect them. You need each other. Your children need each other.

Talk to your children often about how they are doing while daddy is gone. Let them know they can always come to you regardless of the time or what you're involved in. Be sensitive to their emotions and lack of being able to adequately explain why or what they're feeling. If you notice changes in their behavior or health don't neglect it. There are wonderful support groups for children of deployed parents.

Before every deployment, soldiers and their spouses must update all their legal documents and family information. This is a good time to make sure all of your Power of Attorneys are up to date and if you think you may possibly need a specific one, make sure you take care of it before deployment rather than while he's overseas. He needs to be able to stay focused on the mission, but it's more difficult and time consuming to handle such affairs while he's away. Ensure that your family emergency profile is updated and posted on the refrigerator or back of the kitchen door. Confirm your medical insurance is up to date and yours and your children's information is accurately in DEERS (Defense Eligibility Enrollment Reporting System). Know the Red Cross number to reach your husband in case of emergency. I had to rely on this several times and it works fast. You must have your husband's deployment information correct. When our son was born while Hero was in training in another state the Red Cross had him on the phone within an hour. When my grandmother had a heart attack they had Hero on the phone within three hours from Iraq and on a plane home within days. The Red Cross Military Hotline is one to keep handy.

Talk with your husband about what decisions he would rather you seek his approval on and which ones he's OK with you making. It is helpful to set a dollar limit on purchases without his approval. Say you set the limit to $500 and an appliance goes out (which it will most likely go out while he's deployed-Murphy's Law) and it would cost more to repair it than to replace it. Either way it will cost more than the limit so you wait until you hear from your husband before making the decision to repair or replace. Sometimes things can't wait. Ask him how he wants you to handle these things so there is no undue stress. It never failed, within hours of Hero stepping onto that C-130, something broke down or one of the children got sick. Be prepared for it.

Hero and I found that once he got word they were going on mission we both had a tendency to pull away from each other and go into this strange protective mode. We would begin arguing over silly things. It was as if being upset with each other would make the separation easier. Once we realized what was going on, we were able to address it and handle it more wisely. You never really get over the thought of your husband possibly never coming home or returning severely injured. It's just part of the military lifestyle. These things need to be discussed openly and with love. Be careful not to take your concerns out on him. It is his job. Most likely he loves what he does. Accept this and love him even more for it. When you talk with him about your concerns, make sure you don't put any undue pressure on him. He needs to know you'll be OK while he's gone. If you experience severe anxiety or depression talk with one of your girl friends or a Christian counselor. Whatever you do, never go to his higher up or chain of command. This is absolutely not acceptable. Not only will you be embarrassed, but your husband will get in trouble for this. If you have concerns that you feel need to be addressed go to your Chain of Command within the FRG. If your lead person can't help you, then go to the next lady in line. Only if necessary, go to the FRG Leader.

Chain of Command is taken very seriously. By the way, your husband may be the one wearing the uniform, but your whole family is in the military. You have to respect their code of conduct and protocols. Learn the military acronyms, rules, ranks, and Chain of Command. You are representing your husband and how you conduct yourself, both on and off post, is a direct reflection on him. When conducting business on base, know how to address those in uniform and recognize the enlisted from officers. Avoid embarrassing yourself and your man. Trust me, word gets around if you're a problem.

Speaking of representing your husband, dress the part too. Again, how you carry yourself and handle your children is so important. Represent your husband well. Your children need to behave during deployment briefings. Extremely important information is given out, and everyone needs to be able to hear it without your children being a distraction. Carry yourself with respect and poise. Dress the part. Don't show up looking like a prostitute. I promise you, these things matter. Your husband's military career partly relies on how you conduct yourself as a military wife. They don't need soldiers whose wives are causing chaos.

Before deployments, help your husband make sure the house is ready. Check on all appliances, including vehicles. Make sure you are up to speed on regular maintenance schedules. Ensure that all smoke alarms have new batteries and fire extinguishers are up to date. Check that First-Aid kits are fully supplied. If there is anything you need your husband to handle, give him plenty of notice. Remember, he's also preparing himself for deployment. Make his job as easy as possible. He will have a lot on his mind, preparing mentally for battle. You want him at top notch mentality.

During deployments, send your husband lots of care packages with the things he likes. Remember his buddies who may not be married or have family sending them packages. We used to send them fun things too, such as Nerf guns, playing cards, dominoes, miniature basketball goals with ball, board games, etc. They do have down time, and that can be a time of great difficulty and homesickness for them. Send lots of pictures of you and the kids. Keep him up to date with what your family is doing and their accomplishments. Be honest with him about your family's health but without overwhelming or worrying him. Let him know you can handle it. When your husband is able to call, drop what you are doing and focus on him. Let the children talk with him.

Keep track of the days daddy is gone on the calendar. Note milestones of the children. This is for the benefit of the entire family. Not only does it help keep track of major accomplishments for the children, but it is a great family archive of your history and when things happened. Trust me, things will run together and get blurry.

Always have your home ready as if your husband may walk in at any minute. With Special Operations units this was an actual possibility. We were not privy to knowing exactly when they would leave or return. There may be times where he gets a call in the middle of the night and has to leave immediately. He may not be able to tell you why or where he's going, or when he'll return. You have to be OK with this. This is for his safety and that of his comrades. Talk to your children about this reality and include them as much as possible. Let them say good-bye to daddy. Never lie to them about him leaving. Refrain from telling them that he's going on vacation. Be honest with them but respectful of their still developing minds and emotions.

Regarding OPSEC (Operational Security), abide by it. Respect it. Your extended family may not understand it or agree with it. They may feel like they need to know information or that you are being dramatic. It doesn't matter. If you are told not to share certain information about your husband's job or deployments, then don't. This is for his safety and his teammates' safety. You never know who is listening in on phone calls or who may get wind of the information. I remember the wives were banned from going to our local mall, because there was a group who owned kiosk businesses in the hallways. They had connections to the enemy overseas. When our ladies would walk through the mall they would strike up conversation and fish for information on our husbands' jobs, unit, and deployments. This put our men at great risk because many of the women didn't understand the importance of OPSEC or didn't recognize that what these men were doing was attempting to harm our men. This also puts you and your family at risk. We must keep our husbands' security in mind at all times.

When your husband is deployed, set out a couple of pairs of men's boots by the front door. Change up which vehicle you use and where you park them.

Always keep all of your exterior lights on during the night. Make sure your trusted neighbors know your husband is gone and ask them to look out for you. Be cautious to answer your door if you are not expecting anyone. Your friends and family will learn real fast to call before visiting. This is partly for your security but also for your sanity. Let me share a story with you about one of many situations that occurred during deployment.

Being in SOCOM (Special Operations Command), our unit functioned a little differently than regular Army. If our husband was injured or killed overseas more than likely a non-uniformed officer and/or chaplain would arrive with our contact person (This was a friend within battalion who would be notified before you in the event of your husband's casualty or fatality). This friend would most likely show up with or after the notification team. Due to this notification system an unexpected knock on the door could cause quite a stir.

One Saturday morning around 0900hrs, all four kids and I were sitting in the living room. They were watching cartoons and I was working at the computer.

Two black Lincoln Town cars pull up in front of our driveway. They sat there for quite a while. Then four men in black suits stepped out and stood talking in front of our house. One of them had a clipboard in hand. My heart and stomach were twirling inside. I told our oldest daughter to follow the planned protocol of taking the babies upstairs and calling our neighbor to come right away to get the children. She didn't want to go. She sat there with watery eyes, watching the men. I prayed the Lord would help me respond in a way that wouldn't scare the kids. I asked God to help me be strong. Flashes of my future as a single mother raced through my mind. The black suits approached our door. My stomach tied in knots; I thought I was going to be sick. Their knock on the door was amplified and sounded like we were in a tunnel. The pounding came again. I slowly carried myself to the door.

I opened the door and trembled, "Can I help you."

One of the black suits smiled and replied, "We're here to share the good news!"

WHAT??? Is this some kind of sick joke?! "EXCUSE ME?!" I bellowed. I literally wanted to punch this jerk in the throat. I slammed the door in his face. He knocked again. I don't know why, but I answered it.

He stated calmly, almost eerily, "Ma'am, we're here to share the good news. We're Jehovah's Witnesses."

A wave of emotions came crashing over me. What do I do with this? I busted out laughing and sobbing at the same time. The man was very confused.

I looked him square in the eyes and pointed at the "No Soliciting" sign and sternly told him to never come to my door again.

He asked me if everything was all right. I explained the situation. I believe he felt terrible. They never returned. Make sure your family and friends notify you before knocking.

Avoid putting decals on your vehicles that share any personal information about your husband's job, unit or location. Don't put decals that describe your family personally, such as the little people showing how many children you have or decals from your daughter's dance academy or your son's soccer team. Don't put school decals on your vehicle. All of these things tell a story about your family and make you vulnerable. Do not post any details on social media about your husband's deployment or his location. Social media is a major threat to our military and the security of their family. Not only that, it makes you and your children more vulnerable because now they know you're alone. Be smart about protecting your family.

It is wise to learn how to properly protect your family. If you choose to arm yourself and your home, make certain you know how to use the weapon effectively and safely. Ensure your children don't have access to your weapons. Ask your husband to help you prepare and train for situations. My husband used to wake me up in the middle of the night and yell in my ear, "I'm an intruder and just broke in, quick, what are you going to do?" He walked me through how to prepare and defend our home. He showed me where to position myself and our children. Our children were trained at a very young age how to respond, where to go, what to do and not to. They learned that if a one-word command was given they needed to immediately follow orders without speaking. We trained often. All of this information is not meant to scare you or your children, rather to help you be informed and prepared.

There are great courses you can take to help you train for self and home defense. Take them.

When it comes to extended family, keep them informed as much as possible without breaking OPSEC. Especially keep your husband's family informed, namely his mother. She wants to know her baby is alright. Explain to your family as best you can how important security is and that you will keep them informed as much as possible but request they respect the importance of OPSEC. This may require that your family learn not to ask you certain things over the phone, such as deployment departure and return dates and locations. You may even be instructed to refrain from asking about weather conditions or terrain as this can tip off the enemy to their whereabouts. Keep this in mind when talking with your husband when he is able to call. Your calls will most likely be recorded or monitored, and if you bring things up that break OPSEC, don't be surprised if your phone call gets dropped. Hopefully your family will understand and respect the rules.

Military life means learning how to celebrate holidays and important dates any time of year. Because of deployments and training, very seldom will your family get to celebrate Christmas on Christmas Day. You may do a little something with the children for their sake, but the big celebration will most likely be when dad comes home, because he doesn't want to miss out. Have a family vote. Some husbands are alright if you and the children have the full celebration without him and share by video or Face Time. Technology has made deployment so much more manageable. My husband enjoyed participating in celebrations. So the children and I would have a small one on Christmas, but when he returned, we would celebrate big. I remember one year this happened in June. We decorated the outside of our house with lights and decked the inside out. We had our tree up and everything. Our neighbors understood and loved it. I don't think my husband and I were together for our anniversary once in twelve years. To this day we have trouble remembering the day of our anniversary. As a military family you learn to celebrate everyday, especially when your husband is home with you.

Traditions are important for the children but it is also important to teach them that honoring their dad's sacrifice is more important. This may mean delaying a tradition until he is home. Discuss this openly as a family and come to an agreement how traditions will be handled. It may be very fluid and ever changing…this in itself came be a time-cherished tradition. Make your children's lives as normal as possible but also include your husband in family activities and traditions. The main thing to know is that your family time is important, and it doesn't really matter if you celebrate a holiday or special event on a specific day. You can easily celebrate Christmas in June or Easter in December.

While on the discussion of holidays and celebrations this may be a good time to mention the widely known and accepted military rule, "Hurry up and Wait." This is such a true statement and will quickly become your life. If you were not a patient person before, trust me you will be after the military. Your husband will receive orders and your family will plan accordingly only to be told to, "Wait." You may even have your entire house packed if you're doing a DITY (Do it Yourself) move only to be told, not yet, or not there. Your life will become adjusted to a constant state of readiness; for what, you may not know until it happens. Your children need to learn and understand this. Our children learned to become flexible and easily acclimated to whatever situation we were in. Our oldest daughter not only had to change schools her senior year, but we moved to a new home in a new state. She went from a very large urban school to a super tiny, IB charter school in a very wealthy part of town. While she wasn't thrilled with these changes at the time, she looks back and realizes how much she learned from this experience and greatly appreciates it. Military kids are resilient!

One of the best things you can do is train your children to look at every change as an opportunity for adventure. Regardless of where we were moving to or what was changing, instead of focusing on what we might be losing, we focused on the excitement of what we were gaining. We moved from central Texas with minimal water sources to the east coast only minutes from the beach and many rivers. We took time to sight see and learn the new area. We studied the culture and history of the state. One of our houses was on an island about ten minutes from the nearest beach. That year, instead of making snowmen, we made sandmen. We celebrated the holidays with an island twist. We made use of the beaches and delicious seafood restaurants. When we moved back to Texas, we lived on a small ranch in a rural town. We raised sheep, pigs, a horse, and lots of chickens. We learned the country way of life.

Living on the small ranch taught us so many life lessons. Then, we moved again to the central part of the United States. We have experienced beautiful changes of terrain, many water ways, a much slower lifestyle and lots of outdoor activities.

Military life provides so much opportunity, excitement and adventure. You make many friends along the way. Some will be friends for a season and others will be lifelong friends who are there for you anytime. You learn how to make friends quickly, yet cautiously. Meeting people from all walks of life and from all parts of the world affords many learning opportunities for your family. Similarities and differences can be celebrated. Your friends become your family away from home.

I have a final note about parenting during deployment. It can be tempting to assign duties to your children they are not ready for. I encourage you to refrain from telling your son that while dad is away he is the man of the home. First of all, this is simply not true. You are next in the Chain of Command, not your son. This also places undue pressure on your son. I made this mistake in the beginning. I regret that. Try not to make your children feel guilty for stressing you out while daddy is gone. Children may not completely comprehend the stresses that come with deployment. All they know is they want a hug from daddy, but he is not home. As a military family, your life will not look like the average family. How you respond to situations and emotions is very different because of the dynamics of military life. The fact is, your husband is deployed in a dangerous part of the world fighting bad guys. There are very real possibilities of what could happen. People may not understand if you decide to take your kids out of school one day and go to the beach because your child had a "missing daddy" breakdown that morning. Military life is fluid and ever-changing. Most non-military people won't understand or appreciate this. That's OK.

Following is some encouragement from some very special friends:

Christine Best Lister — "Embrace the suck. You're not the first one to go through this and you won't be the last. Spend less time complaining and more time learning. A good Mil-wife knows the military alphabet before her husband gets out of basic."

Dave Marshal — "Embrace the "New Normal."

Sherri Shepherd Thompson — "We lived in the Army of, "If we wanted you to have a wife and kids, we'd have issued them to you" and what I would have given for email, Facebook and all the ways to face time with each other. Letters from CONUS to Korea - 7-10 days each way and phone calls were $1.25/minute (about $3 in today's market). Would I trade any of it? No, because it made us the people we are today. We are strong and independent and we can conquer anything. It brought God into our lives again. We have life skills and knowledge that are invaluable, especially if the 'stuff hits the fan' one day. So my best advice - it isn't an easy life, but it is a gratifying life and enlisted pay is never enough. One other thing I'd say is never, ever tell your kid they are the man/woman of the house while the soldier is gone. Too much responsibility put on a child. Saw many do that."

Wendy Butusov — "Make friends. There will be many holidays and special occasions alone. Prepare for Murphy's Law during deployments or training. Enjoy and explore each duty station…it's home for the next few years. Love and be patient with your kids.... having one parent present is hard enough."

Danielle McDaniels — "Work as a team with your husband, and take pride as being part of that team, you serve a greater purpose and it's easier to endure the hardships when you feel like you're both a valued part of the team and doing something greater than yourself. This life is hard, and it's ok that it's hard. (My favorite quote or saying is, 'This life is tough Sweetheart, but so are you.'). Homecomings are the BEST!! Those are the best hugs and kisses ever! Friends! So important, they become your family, and some will last for life and some will be only for a season. Your marriage will be tested at some point, love each other and give grace. Sometimes (a lot) the needs of the Military come before your relationship, anniversaries, birthdays, holidays, and planned leave, be as flexible and understanding as you can. If he could change it he would. Don't take your anger with military leadership decisions out on your husband, he usually had nothing to do with making that decision and couldn't change it if he tried. Keep Christ the center of your marriage. It puts a lot of things into perspective."

Jennifer Cooley-Beckwith — "You have to be a team partner with your husband at all times. Deployments are hard, especially if you have children. Encourage him and love him through the good, the bad, and the ugly. Most importantly, keep Christ the center of your marriage at ALL times, and I promise you that you'll both do wonderfully. Yes, times can get hard, but with God, all things are possible. Get prepared to move a lot. Find good positive friends; ones that inspire, encourage, and uplift you. Send your husband mail on deployments! That's very important to them. Send cookies, care packages etc. Ask them if others are receiving stuff too because you will be surprised how many other men and women do not get care packages so try to send some extra stuff. Feeling loved from overseas is priceless. Send daily devotionals too. They have to stay on top of God's word while deployed. Most importantly, find a Church family as this will be a HUGE source of comfort. Nothing rocks more than a true Church family. Let your kids be involved as much as they can. Make calendars or jars with something special to count down the days that a parent is gone. I'll fill in and stand in the gap with you for continued prayers and support. Remember God is so amazing and his Grace is sufficient "

Daelynn Williams — "My dad was in the military for 20+ years. Things I learned from my mom—1)Have get-togethers when the husbands are home with other families. Build a network with other wives. This helps with having others who understand, help with child care, etc. 2) Most bases have activities and such for families, go to them. 3) Most divisions or units have an ombudsmen, learn who yours is, this can be one of the wives, and will be a great resource or advocate if you need help. (My mom was one for the enlisted wives on my dad's ships). 4) Learn some basic knowledge about your car, when to get oil changed, how to check the fluids, tires, etc. 5) Write letters or emails often, the guys really need to hear from you. Be honest about missing him, but try not to complain. 6) Take lots of pictures so he feels included in some of what is happening at home."

Military life is very rewarding, emotional, and memorable. Keep the faith. Stay connected. Stay strong. You can do it! God bless you and God bless America.

RECOMMENDED RESOURCES

Love and Logic: They provide a plethora of products and resources on parenting. You can find their materials at www.loveandlogic.com. Their original book is what helped guide me in my parenting when my children were young. Great teachings!

Protecting the Gift: Keeping Children and Teenagers Safe (and Parents Sane)
By: Gavin De Becker

Be Your Own "Doctor"
By: Rachel Weaver M.H.

Backyard Pharmacy
By: Rachel Weaver M.H.

Better Homes and Gardens New Cook Book 11th Edition
By: Meredith

Doterra by Ann Lindholm

HOMESCHOOL CURRICULUM:

www.mfwbooks.com

www.mathusee.com

www.allaboutlearningpress.com (Spelling, reading)

www.rosettastone.com (Foreign language)

www.bluestockingpress.com (Uncle Eric Series)

www.wallbuilders.com (History and government)

OTHER TITLES BY ANN LINDHOLM

Love to Reconcile: The Heart of the Father

Love to Reconcile focuses on healing and reconciliation with the Lord and with others through the act of forgiveness. Practical tools are shared as well as the heart of the Father, which is that all people would be reconciled to Him and with one another.

You can purchase <u>Love to Reconcile</u> in paperback or digital format:
www.authorannlindholm.com

Or, Amazon, Apple Books, Barnes and Noble and other stores.

REVIEWS OF LOVE TO RECONCILE

Jane Saladino-Yoas: Beautifully and lovingly written! Ann reminds us that no sin is bigger than God, and that He loves us no matter what sin we have committed. Ann uses her knowledge and understanding of the Bible to bring us many examples of God's love and forgiveness for us when we repent of our sins. I would recommend this book for anyone who is in need of reconciliation, and who among us isn't?

Brett Crisp: I bought your e-book this morning. I couldn't stop reading. I finished it before I had to go to work. Two words...Absolute Truth!

Jacqueline Bills: The author, Ann Lindholm, did an excellent job revealing the Father's heart from Old Testament all the way through the New Testament with His desire for reconciliation with His children. Using scripture and personal revelation, she brings to light His great love and desire for relationship with every individual. She goes on to share not only His desire for individuals to be in right relationship with Him, but also His desire for our relationships with each other to be reconciled to love and peace and even our nation to be reconciled to God. Ann uses many relevant scriptures to highlight His heart and finishes the book with thought provoking tools to use for application of the reader. Every person, whether far off from God or actively seeking the Lord, will benefit from this book.

Be the first to know about new releases and special events!
Sign up at:
www.authorannlindholm.com

www.ingramcontent.com/pod-product-compliance
Lightning Source LLC
Chambersburg PA
CBHW071351290426
44108CB00014B/1496